Democratic Values
and the Rights of Management

Democratic Values and the Rights of Management

by
Eli Ginzberg and Ivar E. Berg
with
John L. Herma and James K. Anderson

Columbia University Press *New York and London 1963*

Eli Ginzberg is Professor of Economics and Director of the Conservation of Human Resources Project at Columbia University; he is Chairman of the National Manpower Advisory Committee.

Ivar E. Berg is Associate Professor of Business Administration, Columbia University.

James K. Anderson is Director of Personnel, Rockland County, New York.

John L. Herma is a psychotherapist and a member of the Conservation of Human Resources staff.

To Philip Young

Conservation of
Human Resources Project

The Conservation of Human Resources Project was established by General Dwight D. Eisenhower at Columbia University in 1950 to undertake basic research in human resources. It has been supported by grants from corporations, foundations, and the federal government. Dr. Lawrence H. Chamberlain, the Vice-President of the University, exercises administrative supervision over the Project.

Preface

Since the Foreword sets this study within the framework of the research which we are conducting under the Conservation of Human Resources Project, we need consider here only a few of its operational aspects.

In selecting the arbitration awards which form the backbone of Chapters 4 through 8, we studied and evaluated a total of approximately 500 cases. We have cited just under 100 awards; all made since the end of World War II. We chose those which provided a broad coverage of industries and unions and included particularly those in which the arbitrator set out at considerable length the reasons underlying his decision. We also attempted to include decisions of those arbitrators who were recognized as leaders in the field.

The subjects which we covered in analyzing the rights of management were selective. Although we might profitably have considered additional dimensions of the problem, ours was an exploratory study and we deliberately eschewed any attempt at comprehensiveness.

Professor Ivar Berg, principal co-author of this work, joined our group largely because his experience in developing a new core course on "The Conceptual Foundations of Business" in the Graduate School of Business had indicated the inadequacy of materials on the theme of the changing rights and functions of American management. It was his hope that our research would help meet a serious pedagogic need. We anticipate that it will.

Some books can be written only on the basis of ready access to other books. This is such a book. It was our good fortune that Mr. Ben Driver, Business Librarian of Columbia University, believes that a librarian should be an active teammate of the researcher. He assisted us in a great many ways.

Mr. Saul Wallen, my friend and summer neighbor, was a source of strength and reassurance. From the earliest stages of the project he indicated a genuine enthusiasm for this foray into his territory by a group of academic interlopers. And, when the manuscript was finished, he went over it with great care and improved it by additions, subtractions, and corrections. We could not have had a more constructive critic and we deeply appreciate his help.

The style of this manuscript reflects, in the first instance, the simplicity and clarity that characterizes most of the awards which we have cited. It further reflects the skillful editing of Ruth Szold Ginzberg.

ELI GINZBERG, *Director*
Conservation of Human Resources Project

Columbia University
January, 1963

Foreword

This is a study of the way in which the traditional and emergent values of a democracy help to bring about alterations in the behavior of men in the world of work. The analysis is based on the published decisions of arbitrators who have settled disputes between management and labor under collective bargaining agreements. Recent developments underscore the potentialities inherent in this approach. Within the past few months, the Supreme Court upheld a decision of the Second Circuit Court of Appeals which held that the seniority right which workers had earned under a collective bargaining agreement survived the termination of the contract and that an employer had to respect these rights even if he relocated his plant in a new and distant location. He was not free to hire new workers in the new locality; at least, he could not do so until he had offered his former employees their old jobs. The full impact of this new doctrine is yet to be felt as management and unions seek to take it into account in reaching new agreements, and as arbitrators must decide the problematic issues that will inevitably arise in these agreements.

The termination of the long strike by the Order of Railway Telegraphers against the Chicago and Northwestern Railway left many issues to be settled by the arbitrator. The brotherhoods sought to establish an ironclad procedure governing the recall of men to work but their claim was not upheld because the arbitrator emphasized that he would not agree to stripping management of its basic initiative in its search for efficiency. The parameters of managerial initiative are a constant concern of arbitrators as they seek to fill the effective balance between management's rights and workers' equities.

The Darlington Mills Case, now on appeal in the courts, presents yet another dimension of the tangled skein. The National Labor Relations Board decided in this landmark case that management is not at liberty to close a plant because a union has won recognition and seeks to establish working conditions which management considers uneconomic. Management continues to have the right to close down uneconomic units but it cannot take such drastic action in response to a union's victory without first demonstrating that the gains for the workers will in fact result in actual not putative losses. The question of good faith in collective bargaining, as in all contractual relations, is fundamental for the continuing progress of a free economy and a democratic society. This, too, is an issue around which the decisions of many arbitrators revolve.

While arbitration awards and the courts' interpretation of them provide the raw materials for this study, it is not in any sense a study of arbitration or of collective bargaining. To present the focus of this investigation we will recount briefly its origins and delineate the range of considerations which fall within and outside its purview.

We first became aware that changes in social values have an effect on the performance of men in large organizations during our study of the utilization of military manpower in World War II, which was published in 3 volumes in 1959 under the title, *The Ineffective Soldier: Lessons for Management and the Nation.* A detailed review of the disposition of thousands of cases of soldiers whose performance had been called into question revealed that, despite the overriding emergency of war and the national commitment to victory, many decisions were made more with an eye to assuring equity for the serviceman than with concern for the efficiency of the Army. The actions taken by the Army in World War II in dealing with the soldier were different from the policies which it followed in World War I, the shifts reflecting primarily changes in the value structure of the American community. Time and again, military tribunals, in assessing the responsibility of an individual soldier for his effectiveness or wrongdoing, gave weight to such considerations as whether the soldier was suffering from mental incapacity, physical exhaustion, emotional disturbance, or other circumstances or conditions that might help to explain if not justify his default and which should therefore lead to a mitigation in punishment. We saw that in the eyes of the American people the Army had an obligation, even in the midst of a major war, to deal with the citizen-soldier in the light of accepted democratic values.

Alerted to this important theme of the impact of dominant social values on the performance of important organizations we thought it best to continue our explorations within a civilian setting where the findings were likely to have more direct applicability to our dynamic society. While searching for an appropriate body of materials to pursue our analysis, the suitability of arbitration decisions for this purpose of studying the impact of social values on organizational performance was suggested to us by the late Professor Benjamin Selekman of the Harvard Business School. Here was a large body of written materials dealing with conflict situations arising out of the search of the individual for equity and the drive of the organization for efficiency.

We might have found other materials equally suitable for our purpose, such as the decisions of the courts in cases which reflect conflicts in social values. We might have considered the awards of Workmen Compensation Boards. We could have appraised the reports of deans of students, wardens of prisons, or others in leadership positions in large organizations. But these alternatives had no clear advantage over the decisions of arbitrators and in fact they did not appear to offer as much range and depth as we knew to exist in the arbitration process.

Every choice has drawbacks as well as advantages. In deciding to study the awards of arbitrators, we considered the argument that with the trade union movement accounting for a declining proportion of the labor force the significance of arbitration was waning. We decided, however, that it is premature to reach firm conclusions about the future of the trade union movement from the trends in membership during the last decade. In the past, periods of slow growth or even decline have been followed by renewed expansion. There is no reason to rule out the repetition of such a pattern.

In any case, even if the trade union movement were to remain on a plateau or actually decline, the issues to which arbitrators have addressed themselves in years past involving conflicts between the worker and management would still be relevant. Our contemporary system of arbitration is embedded in the collective bargaining agreements between managements and unions, but even without such agreements, employers and employees would still have to find a mutually satisfactory way for settling the multitude of conflicts that inevitably arise in any large organization where management's primary concern is with efficiency and the employee is jealous of protecting his rights and freedom. And any alternative method for adjudicating such conflicts would inevitably be sensitive to the value structure of the society. Professor Selznick and his associates at the University of California have been clarifying the inevitab:lity in a democratic society that the rule of law will permeate industry. In fact, the compulsion goes beyond a democratic society; in both Soviet Russia and Spain, mechanisms have been developed for resolving conflicts in the work place.

We also considered the argument that arbitration is simply one aspect of an ongoing and ceaseless power struggle between management and the union which also includes contract negotiations, strikes, agreements, grievance procedures and the implicit bargaining in the shop as was recently reviewed again by our colleague, Professor James Kuhn. It is sometimes held that the cases that come to arbitration—as well as those which do not—reflect the changing pressures exerted on management and union officials. More frequently than not the partners to the contract find it politically expedient or otherwise to their mutual advantage to process certain grievances to the point where they go to arbitration. Often, these cases appear to be trivial.

We considered a further contention that since the arbitrator's survival depends on his maintaining the confidence of both parties, his overriding concern is to establish a record which demonstrates his impartiality. No matter what rationale he may use in his opinions, his main concern is to strive for a balance in his awards. He must be sensitive not only to the needs of management to operate efficiently but also to the rights that workers have obtained as a result of an agreement. There is virtue in the arbitrator seeking to narrow the differences between contestants. The vitality of a democracy and the efficiency of its economy depends not on abstract justice but on compromise and consensus.

A further argument might be that many arbitrators have begun to make a career of arbitrating and that wittingly or unwittingly they are engaged in "make-work." Confronted with lack of clarity in the terms of the contract, they build on and elaborate the ambiguities rather than directing their efforts to forcing the parties to clarify and sharpen the terms of the agreement when next they have an opportunity. There is nothing to prevent the parties from so doing but if they continue to leave ambiguities which invite arbitration they may be making a deliberate and even a sound choice.

We considered the substance of the awards. Margaret Chandler has argued persuasively in her exhaustive analysis of "contracting-out" that the exigencies of a dynamic economy are such that no matter what the arbitrator may decide in any specific case, management must eventually have its way. The imperatives of private enterprise are so overwhelming that if the logic of production or distribution demands that an employer contract out in order to enhance his efficiency, it will only be a matter of time before the union is forced to acquiesce. Dr. Chandler has pointed to the growing opportunities that an aggressive management now has to play off one union against another. The burden of her conclusions, to be published in 1963, is a warning against exaggerating the importance of the victories that unions win from arbitration. These victories can be turned into defeats when a new contract is negotiated. To recognize that management, especially in the long run, retains a high order of initiative is not to deny entirely the significance of workers' rights protected in the short run. For the long run is made up of a series of short runs.

In all judicial or semi-judicial procedures, the question of remedy is of major importance. A decision or an award is unimportant unless it provides for an effective remedy. It has been claimed that all too frequently the workers' victory is limited to rhetoric, neither the arbitrator nor the court provides an effective remedy. This is undoubtedly true. But a union learns from hollow victories. Next time round, it will seek to write into the agreement valid remedies.

One other disadvantage could be cited against basing a study of the impact of social values on industrial life on arbitration awards. The arbitrator's decisions which are published represent a selection from a much larger, unknown universe. This means that there is no way of assessing the biases contained in the published materials. There is no certainty even as to precedent. Surely the decisions which appear in print represent for the most part cases which have some special merit in that they raise new issues or present old issues evaluated in a novel manner. Moreover, the published decisions heavily represent those rendered by the leading practitioners. The prevailing penchant for quantitative studies should not obscure the importance of other approaches. Rich case materials usually permit probing to deeper levels of meaning. The ways in which leading arbitrators approach and resolve complex cases may be more illuminating to study than tabulating their decisions. Nor can one ignore the fact that the Supreme Court is willing to make new law on many crucial issues even without having before it tests of statistical significance covering arbitration awards.

This, then, is our justification for developing a study from arbitration records even though trade union membership may be declining, many of the cases that go to arbitration appear to be trivial, arbitrators frequently seem to split their awards, much of their work has the appearance of make-work, many awards won by labor have no effective remedy, and the inherent biases in published decisions cannot be evaluated.

Now that we have identified these questions with respect to the suitability of arbitration awards as the raw materials of an inquiry into the role of values in industrial life, it is important to recall our earlier caveat. This book is not a study of arbitration or of collective bargaining. Many of the problems on which it focusses are at the periphery of the power struggle between management and the union. They involve conflicts between the organization and the individual worker and the awards frequently involve neither binding precedent nor heavy costs.

Not all management-labor conflicts are struggles for survival; many fall within a broad arena where the major interests of the principal participants are not in jeopardy. They arise out of a lack of congruence between management's continuing exercise of its prerogative to improve its efficiency and the individual worker's continuing search for equity.

Irrespective of whether the conflicts and the ensuing awards involve peripheral or vital interests of the contestants, and irrespective of the wide range of considerations that may play a part in the arbitrator's decision, the fact remains that the rationale of his decision has a significance of its own. He has been chosen by both parties to weigh their respective claims and to render a judgment which enables the firm to pursue profits through greater efficiency and, at the same time, protects the rights of the workers under the contract. Since conflicts cannot be avoided and since the principals cannot resolve them without recourse to trials of strength, the arbitrator performs an essential task. In discharging it, he must seek to persuade both parties that his awards are reasonable. In this effort, he must rely on what Secretary of Labor Wirtz has called the "arbitrament of reason." The ideas which the arbitrator puts forward and the language in which he clothes them are his only allies. But they are powerful allies when well deployed since most men, even in the heat of economic battle, are open to influence and

persuasion, especially by one whom they have chosen and respect.

In the face of opposition, most men realize that there may
be some right to the other side and unless their most vital interests are at stake they are usually willing to abide by the judgment of an independent judge. If, as in arbitration, they know
that the arbitrator who will hear the case and render the decision understands the realistic conditions under which work
is carried out, they will accept his conclusion. The arbitrator
in turn realizes that his decision will be more fully accepted if
he is able to illuminate facets of the conflict that have not been
completely understood by the contestants and to assess them in
light of the established and emerging values of the larger society.
Employers and employees alike are part of this larger society and
participate as citizens in shaping it. Consequently they appreciate the arbitrator's recourse to such broader values which they
themselves have helped to establish or at least have accepted
as members of a democratic society.

It is characteristic of a dynamic society that old values are
discarded, and new ones fashioned. But in a pluralistic society
such as ours the transformation of values does not proceed
evenly in all sectors. Sometimes established values are discarded
in one arena and remain entrenched in others. But, if men have
multiple allegiances and affiliations, man is one. Although a
complex industrial community is subdivided into major segments—political, economic, social, and still others—the segments nevertheless must be meaningfully related to each other
for this is a precondition for a viable society. Contradictions in
values build up pressures for change.

There are many different ways of studying how the extension
of social values help to bring about changes in the industrial

arena. In this book, the focus will be on the way in which values of the larger society are reflected back into the work place through the decisions of arbitrators. We shall pay attention both to the arbitrator's constructions of the contract and to his dicta. While arbitrators begin by constructing a contract, they frequently are forced to fill out the interstices, as was recently pointed out anew by a leading arbitrator, Saul Wallen, in an address to The National Academy of Arbitrators, "The Silent Contract vs. Express Provisions." The dicta of arbitrators are often more revealing than their constructions in pinpointing the values on which their decisions finally come to rest. And this book is, above all else, a study of the impact of social values on industrial change.

Contents

PART ONE

PROPERTY VERSUS PEOPLE

1. Extension of Democratic Values

In the tradition of the West, democracy has conventionally been defined in political terms—that is, in terms of the relation of the individual to government. When all, or almost all, adult citizens participate in the process of selecting representatives who are charged with the responsibility for legislating, including the levying of taxes, democracy is said to prevail. It does not follow necessarily that every voter has exactly the same weight as every other in determining governmental policy. As modern conservatives as Judge Manion and Senator Goldwater insist on emphasizing, the United States is a constitutional republic in which each state, irrespective of the number of its inhabitants, shares equally in sending representatives to the upper legislative chamber of the federal government; and, further, each state, within certain limits, can determine for itself the conditions under which the members of its legislature are chosen. In terms of formal structure, American democracy is limited by the separation of powers within the federal government, by the reserved powers of the states, and by the basic rights retained by the individual under constitutional guarantees.

When attention is shifted from structure to functioning the limitations on democracy become much more significant. As the current struggle over Civil Rights has so clearly demonstrated, various pressures have long been exercised to prevent Negroes in the South from voting. And powerful city machines have repeatedly been caught in the act of ballot stuffing. More subtle, but still highly relevant, is the influence exercised by the owners of the communications industries through presenting biased accounts of the candidates and the issues so as to enhance the prospects of their favorites. An effective democracy presupposes an electorate with reasonable access to the facts and with reasonable competence to judge them.

The influence of powerful interests is not limited to the legislative arena but likewise finds expression in the two other branches of government, in the executive and the judiciary. These pressures frequently reflect the interests of particular minority groups; and, while the impact of these groups on the majority may be favorable, it may well be neutral or negative. The last formal address of President Eisenhower just prior to turning over his office to his successor warned about a new and dangerous alliance between the military and defense contractors that threatened to undermine civilian leadership and control of the federal government; and thereby to place in jeopardy the future of American democracy.

The American political system, then, despite the fact that it represents the oldest democracy among the larger nations of the world, has not succeeded in curing all of the defects and blemishes with which it started; in addition, it has acquired some along the way.

Political freedom is a necessary but not a sufficient condition for human freedom. As Anatole France pointed out many years ago, it makes little sense to argue that both the rich man and the poor man are equally free to sleep on the park bench. During the Great Depression of the early 1930s, many women in New York City accepted an offer of fifty cents a day for ten hours of housework, for they had no other way of providing food for their children. And many an unemployed man rummaged in garbage cans to find something to eat.

This crisis helped to bring home to the entire country the lesson that many poor farmers, stranded coal miners, unemployed lumberjacks, unskilled immigrants, steel and cotton hands in company towns, and others had long known: if one must spend most of his waking hours working for somebody else in order to earn enough to purchase the essentials of life, the only freedom that remains, apart from protest or revolt, is to accept existing conditions or starve.

The economic preconditions of American democracy have not received the attention that they deserve. Since land was available for the taking, a man with an axe could be self-supporting. He did not have to be beholden to any other man for his livelihood. And so the interdependence between private property in land and democracy in the political arena was taken largely for granted. While the framers of the Constitution were deeply concerned about reconciling property rights and popular suffrage, the extent to which political freedom presupposes a reasonable degree of economic independence was frequently ignored. Starting with the Feuerbach premise that "man is what he eats," Marx was able to level some of his strongest guns against the unreality of freedom in a capitalistic world by emphasizing that workers who could earn their bread only by selling their labor power to industrialists who controlled all the means of production were vulnerable to all manner of exploitation.

Adam Smith had recognized many years before Marx that competition could be relied upon to yield significant social benefits only to the extent that there was some proximate equality of bargaining power between competing individuals and groups. He pointed out that in the event of labor strife employers were much more able to close down a plant even for a long period while workers had to win quickly or starve since they had no comparable resources to draw on. The rights of strikers to draw unemployment benefits after a waiting period has markedly increased their capacity to engage in a long strike.

It could be argued that rather than ignoring the interdependence of private property and political freedom, the basic structure of our laws and government failed to make a sharp distinction between them. It is as much the obligation of government to protect a man's property as it is to protect his life. For his freedom has point and meaning only to the extent that what he labors to produce and earn is secure from arbitrary seizure or sequestration. As long as most Americans were independent farmers, and as long as free land was available to all who were willing to work it, there were good and sufficient reasons for government and law dedicated to human freedom to protect the individual's person, including his right to vote and his right to enjoy and dispose of his property. The exercise of each right strengthened the other. The colonists rose up against the mother country when they were subjected to taxation without represesentation. For a man was not truly free if the results of his labor could be taken from him without his having any voice in the method of levying or disposing of taxes. While there were poor men, indentured servants, and slaves in the colonies, the gradations in wealth and power among a population predominantly composed of independent farmers were not extreme and all but the slave had a reasonable prospect of gaining, sooner or later, his basic economic independence and political freedom. Since the slave was property, his personal status could not be problematic. His only chance to gain freedom legally was through manumission. As the conflict over slavery deepened, even this route was frequently closed by legislative enactment and social pressures.

The growth of industrialization predicated on the advances of technology and assisted by the development of the limited liability corporation altered fundamentally our eighteenth-century agrarian society and with it the economic foundations on which our system of political democracy had been constructed. The first major step was Chief Justice Marshall's opinion in the Dartmouth College case whereby the corporation was granted the right to be treated as a person to hold property and to make contracts. Later, state legislation approved the granting of charters to corporations and provided for limited liability. And finally, under the Supreme Court's interpretations of the Fourteenth Amendment, the "due process clause" was found applicable to corporations. By the latter half of the nineteenth century, the economic underpinnings of early American democracy had been all but eroded. Powerful combinations and trusts, representing tremendous aggregations of capital, stood against the needs and aspirations of the nation's farmers and workers. In their desire for power and profits, men, families, and communities were frequently ground under heel, and a mockery was made of human freedom.

There were many who argued that while it was regrettable that some people were victimized by the rush towards industrialization, progress always carried a price tag, and it was against natural precepts and democratic principles to attempt to restrict and restrain the wealthy from using their wealth to accumulate more wealth. For was not private property the foundation stone of American democracy? And had not the country declared that corporations were persons whose contractual and property rights could not arbitrarily be altered?

In the post Civil War era laissez-faire won out. The leaders of both major parties became committed to the doctrine that competition represented the best system for allocating scarce resources and rewarding people according to their contribution to meeting basic human needs. As John Bates Clark, the leader of the neoclassical school of economists, emphasized shortly before the turn of this century, everybody receives exactly what he is worth. But it was not many years later that Clark, having reached the conclusion that the competitive market could not be relied upon to discipline the giants in the public interest, wrote a book on *The Control of Trusts* in collaboration with his son, John Maurice Clark.

While big business left few stones unturned to control those who made and interpreted the laws, the gross distortions of American life and liberty which resulted from the onrushing industrialization were more than many could accept, and slowly, opposing forces began to gain strength. The counterattack moved on two major fronts—the political and the economic. The passage of the Sherman Anti-Trust Act in 1890 represented, if not in intent at least by later juridical interpretation, a barrier to the continued aggregation of capital, for a limitation was placed on the corporation's freedom of contract if the intent or the result of its actions were to monopolize the market. Further restrictions and restraints through legislation resulted from efforts to establish minimum conditions of employment. While state and federal courts declared many of these statutory efforts unconstitutional under the doctrine that they represented an infringement of the right of a person (corporation or individual) to determine freely the conditions under which they were willing to offer employment or to accept it, some of the statutes were upheld as measures supportive of the health and safety of the country—including the welfare of children not yet born.

But the counterattack was not limited to action along the legislative front. While workmen had been organizing themselves into unions since the beginning of the nineteenth century for the purposes of negotiating terms of employment with owners of capital and of developing various schemes of self-help, only a small number of effective labor organizations had been established and fewer still had been able to maintain and expand their membership with the passage of years. Initially, their progress was slowed by hostile employers and antagonistic courts; later, by the increased mobility of the work force and radical alterations in the pattern of work. Then the speedy collapse, after the spectacular growth, of the Knights of Labor, with its overtly radical political goals, left the larger community antagonistic and the ranks of labor in confusion. But, by the 1880s and 1890s, a new effort to organize was getting under way—this time with the more limited but practical aim of establishing in different trades some order of control over the supply of labor, the allocation of jobs, and the wage structure. After several decades of freewheeling expansion during which they succeeded increasingly in controlling legislatures, courts, press, and public, the leaders of industrial capitalism encountered opposition. Their reactions were intense. Employers saw the rise of unions as nothing more nor less than an effort to rob them of their property and they sought and secured the support of the police and courts to beat back the challenge of labor. The intensity of their response was heightened by their realization that if unions succeeded in their organizing effort the loss would be permanent, not temporary.

The bloodiness of many organizing struggles also reflected the workers' awareness that if they were ever to know a meaningful freedom, they must secure a voice in determining the conditions under which they worked and the wages they received for their labor. It further reflected the awareness of employers that successful unionization would inevitably result in limiting their freedom of action and decision, in raising the level of wages, and consequently in reducing the profits that they could earn on their investment.

As the struggle over organization went on, it was frequently associated with varying degrees of physical assault, bloodshed, and death, for both parties realized that they were playing for high stakes. The trade union organizers had the difficult task of convincing workers that if they would get together and challenge the boss, they stood to make a whole series of gains, but workers were hard to persuade because they were more conscious of the immediate risks than of long-term advantages. They worried about loss of income, dismissal, loss of home, blacklisting, as well as physical injury and even death. They knew that if they went out on strike, their wages and their credit at the store would cease, they would probably be evicted from the company house, and it was even likely that their employer would import thugs to beat them up and, if necessary, shoot them down.

From today's vantage point, it is possible to delineate the major lines of the struggle with relative sharpness. Employers fought the efforts of labor to unionize, usually with all the weapons at their disposal—economic, legal, political, and criminal. Many had inherited wealth. Others, by dint of hard work, ability, and luck, had succeeded in amassing large fortunes. Our society placed a high value on the successful businessman—in fact the highest. What is more, the prevailing ideology emphasized that the welfare of the society depended on the acumen and skill with which the businessman managed his business. In protecting his patrimony, the businessman was contributing to the continued growth and well-being of the nation. Only a man without character would fail to fight for what was rightfully his—not only in his view but also in the view of his peers. Many employers, enjoying the fruits of a long expansion and prosperity, were willing to grant concessions to their workers but they were unalterably opposed to being forced to negotiate with them. Their business was theirs; they were responsible for its success; they alone would determine what, if anything, they would do for their workers beyond what the law ordered and the market forced them to do.

But the employer's intransigence ran headlong into an increasingly aggressive position held by the more self-conscious sector of the laboring population. The labor view also was grounded in a basic commitment to freedom, the freedom of the individual worker-citizen. The leaders of labor emphasized that the establishment and protection of human freedom, basic to the American tradition, could be realized only if men and women were not forced to live and work under conditions in which they were subject to the arbitrary demands of their employers. Where was freedom for men who had to work from sunup to sundown, constantly exposed to dangerous machinery, who if injured were discharged without compensation, and who, if they failed to knuckle under to the slightest whim of their boss, were subject to instant dismissal, no matter how long or how good their prior record of employment. This was industrial slavery and industrial slavery could never be compatible with political democracy.

And so the conflict was joined—a conflict between the protection of property and the expansion of human rights. While the conflict was relentless and bloody, it was not unlimited. Except for a small and hopelessly splintered minority on the extreme left, American labor did not challenge the fundamentals of industrial capitalism. Rather, it accepted the system and sought to modify its operation. As we found in one of our earlier investigations, visitors from abroad were repeatedly amazed by the fact that the bloodiest types of labor conflict were usually suc-

ceeded by relative calm. Having worked out, at least for some
time ahead, a basis of accommodation, the parties who had been
in violent conflict were able to get together and get on
with the job of producing goods—on which better wages,
higher profits, and improved opportunities for both sides depended.

The absence of feudal institutions, the fact that the nation
had won its freedom through revolution, the heterogenity of
the ethnic groups that came to settle, the plentitude of free
land, the rapid rate of economic development—all contributed
to a higher order of fluidity in American society. The old South,
both before and after the Civil War, was the one exception.
There, class and caste antagonisms dominated. Elsewhere, the
combined forces of political democracy and social and economic mobility prevented the development of deep class cleav-
ages.

It may be helpful to consider in brief outline the major forces
that appear to have brought about basic pacification. World
War I gave national political recognition to organized labor,
and this helped to raise its self-esteem and speed its acceptance
by the public. The restrictive immigration legislation of the
early 1920s, in the passage of which labor played a major role,
foreshadowed that in the not distant future most workers would
be native born and, therefore, would be more sensitive to wide
discrepancies between the goals of a democratic society and the
conditions of their own lives. The potential for dissatisfaction
was also rising as a result of a steady advance in the average
level of schooling.

Changes were also taking place on the employer front. There
are a spate of recent studies that point up the fact that many
businessmen who had risen to the top had not fought their
way there but had had their leadership passed on to them by

their fathers and grandfathers. In many large corporations, a hired management had taken over the controls. While sweeping generalizations would not be in order, it is probably correct to say that on balance the younger generation of business leaders were somewhat less hostile to the claims of unions; at least, many of them would not resort to the same weapons to fight a challenge to their authority. They had grown up and had been educated in decades in which the whole of the Western world had become aware of, and responsive to, the rights of the workingman to reasonable conditions of employment and income. And a small number of sophisticated employers perceived that the worst fears of their confreres about the impact of unionization had been proven false. It was possible to deal with a union and continue to run one's own business efficiently and continue to make large profits. The decline in union membership during the 1920s bespoke the strength of these new forces. It also reflected the reasonably satisfactory wages and working conditions that had come to characterize large sectors of American industry as a result of competitive forces reinforced by the awareness of many industrialists that the best way to prevent the growth of unions was to provide conditions equal to or better than those established under collective bargaining labor agreements.

The situation was more or less at a standstill in the late 1920s; relatively few unions were strong; the union movement was weak. Then came the Great Depression which witnessed the undermining of the entire economy to a point where the future of both unions and corporate enterprise was in jeopardy. The economic holocaust undermined for the first time the faith of labor as well as many other citizens in the future of industrial capitalism. The ability of capitalism to meet its primary requirement of providing jobs and wages had been found wanting. There was no longer any reason to hold back from radical changes.

As the presidential election of 1932 made clear and the election of 1936 confirmed, the vast majority of the American public was ready for a New Deal. And, in the radical readjustments that characterized the first three years of the Roosevelt administration, labor succeeded in making use of the political machinery to help it accomplish what it had struggled for so long and so hard to do on its own—to organize many sectors of the economy which had held out, particularly the mass production industries. The passage of the National Labor Relations Act (Wagner Act) in 1935 was the watershed. But the full implications of the new legislation were only slowly revealed as the Act was interpreted by board members who were sympathetic to altering the balance of power in the relations of management and labor.

A quarter of a century has passed since the law of the land stipulated that management must bargain collectively with representatives of the workers of their own choosing. It has been for the most part a quarter century of high level employment, marked increases in money and real income, rapidly advancing wage rates, the expansion of fringe benefits, and substantial reductions in the hours of labor. A few economists, such as Milton Friedman of the University of Chicago, argue that unions had little if anything to do with these developments for they reflect in the first instance war mobilization, an inflationary policy engendered by governmental spending, relative shortages in the supply of labor, and other forces that transcend the scale and scope of union power. Professor E. H. Chamberlin of Harvard and others, however, see unions as largely responsible for the inflation, the creeping unemployment, the more vulnerable international competitive position of the American economy, and other untoward trends. While it is beyond the purview of this study to assess the relative merits of these positions, it is difficult to see how the truth can lie anywhere but in between, for, clearly, trade unions had sufficient power to influence in some degree many of these outcomes, and, clearly, they did not have sufficient power to determine these outcomes exclusively.

Having taken note of the success of organization in the years immediately preceding the outbreak of World War II, it is necessary for us to return to our major theme and to review the next order of accommodation that occurred as labor sought to increase its influence over the terms of employment.

Organization was not, of course, an end in itself but simply a means to the end whereby employers could be forced to negotiate with their employees in setting the basic terms of employment, particularly those dealing with wages, hours, and what has come to be subsumed under the term seniority. The latter had long been of central concern to American workers; for once the employer accepted a formal system of seniority, his arbitrary power over who was to be hired, trained, promoted, and, in the event of a reduction in the work force, discharged or laid off and called back was greatly curtailed. The acceptance of seniority, next to the recognition of the union itself, represented the most important shift of power over the control of the work arena. The employer was no longer free to make all of the decisions about the recruitment, use, enlargement, or reduction of his work force. Once he committed himself to formal procedures, he could not deviate from them without cause. He could no longer award some and punish others in terms of their acquiescence or hostility to his policies. The worker had gained a major new right which greatly enhanced his economic freedom—a right to his job as long as his job existed, as long as he performed competently and did not get into trouble.

While wages, hours, and seniority represent the basic elements in an employment agreement, there are literally an infinite number of issues on which management and the workers may find themselves in disagreement and conflict. Large-scale industry requires a more or less minute regulating of the work relationship among workers and between workers and superiors. Careful articulation is the basis for efficiency in production. Long before the advent of unions, when the productive structure was much less intricate and subdivided, every work place had work rules which governed informally a great many aspects of how work was to be carried on, including usually such matters as assignments, work loads, rest periods, the handling of emergencies in the life of the individual or of the shop, spoilage, overtime, and many other situations where both the employer and the employee had need to know ahead of time how such issues would be handled. Even in a slave economy, such rules could not be dispensed with.

As long as the employer's power had not been limited by his entering into a contract with a union, the only restraints on his establishing new work rules or modifying old ones were the law—there came a time when he could no longer whip his recalcitrant employees; the market place, since disgruntled employees could leave; and his conscience, which inclined many, though by no means all employers, to overlook errors and shortcomings in employees who had served them well.

While employers and labor accept the necessity, when bargaining periodically breaks down, of resorting to a strike to settle the major terms of a contract, neither side can contemplate relying on the strike as a mechanism for settling the very large number of minor disagreements that inevitably arise in a modern work situation. In fact, they do not even resort to strikes very often in reaching agreements about the basic terms of employment. In 1961, there were a total of about 3,370 work stoppages, involving about 1,450,000 workers. In total, workers were idle for about 16.3 million workdays which amounted to about .14 of 1 percent of total working time.

Since the employer who had signed an agreement with a union was no longer in a position to make unilateral determinations concerning conflicts which arose, some mechanism had to be evolved for the handling of grievances under conditions that would assure that they would be taken up, evaluated, and decided expeditiously and fairly. Recourse to arbitration appeared to be the answer. The last several decades have seen the rapid institutionalizing of arbitration.

In a landmark decision in 1960, the Supreme Court in the case of the *Warrior and Gulf Navigation Co. v. the United Steel Workers* adumbrated the view that arbitration is the fulcrum of collective bargaining on which rests the entire system of industrial self-government. If a collective bargaining agreement provides for arbitration, and more particularly if labor has agreed not to resort to strikes during the course of the agreement, then the view of the Supreme Court appears to be that almost every conflict that arises between the parties is arbitrable except for the few that may have been explicitly excluded by terms of the agreement.

The first and overwhelming objective of arbitrators is to resolve the conflicts that arise under the agreement in a manner that will facilitate continued operations without contributing to intensified conflicts in the future. Since no contract or agreement can ever be completely self-enforcing and since agreements between management and labor cannot possibly cover explicitly more than a small percentage of all contingencies, the need for interpretation cannot be circumvented. The arbitrator is under compulsion to guide himself by the written contract.

It is not his province to alter the basic agreement. But it is inevitable that during the course of an agreement, issues will arise that will allow, in fact demand, that the arbitrator break new ground. He is the fulcrum for balancing management's claims about the exigencies of efficiency against workers' claims about human rights and dignity.

The basic terms of the contract reflect in the first instance the power position of the contestants. Arbitration is the new social instrument that we have developed to provide for the resolution of the myriad of conflicts that may arise during the life of a contract which need not be settled by a test of strength. Once the employer was no longer in a position to make all of the rules and regulations governing the terms of employment, some alternative had to be devised. Collective bargaining, with arbitration, has been the country's answer.

The arbitrator's decisions are the case law of industry or, in Justice Douglas's words, the "common law of the shop." And, in the Anglo-Saxon tradition, case law has long been the instrument whereby judges have sought to reconcile the inheritance of the past with the aspirations for the future. Arbitrators, like judges, have a responsibility to balance the necessity for managerial efficiency with the workers' aspirations for security and dignity.

In seeking firm ground for their decisions, arbitrators rely not only on their interpretation of the agreement, the imperatives of industry, and on the common law of the shop but also on the dominant values in the larger society. The arbitrator, by having recourse to these changing social values, helps to speed their infusion into the work place and he thereby contributes to the extension of democracy in industrial life.

2. *Imperatives of Managing*

For several years, business leaders have publicly bemoaned the fact that they no longer possess the prerogatives of management that characteristically were part of the tradition of Western capitalism. They claim that their management rights have been "eroded;" that the unions, arbitrators, and government have been responsible for this erosion; and that this trend presages the collapse of the prevailing economic system which is after all, predicated on the right and the duty of managers to manage.

Occasionally, these arguments have included an element of self-blame. Some leaders have recognized that their representatives have agreed at the bargaining table with unions to terms that later became the instrument of their undoing. Others have warned that as a result of this lack of insight, business may soon arrive at a situation where management will be faced with the obligation of managing without any longer possessing the rights and authority which alone can enable it to perform its task effectively.

Without accepting or denying the validity of the foregoing interpretation of recent trends in business management it is reasonable to postulate that an untoward chain of events has evoked the prevailing view of the dominant group of businessmen today—a view that management's authority is being rapidly eroded and that inherent in the continuance of this trend is the inevitable collapse of the system of free enterprise.

No one can be sure what the future holds in store. But it is frequently helpful to review major transformations that have occurred in a basic institution in order to deepen perspective on its structure and operations and to see more clearly how it has responded to the pushes and pulls of history. The current discussions on management's prerogatives cover a wide range of topics. They include management's rights, management's functions, the imperatives of the capitalistic market, the interdependence of economic and political freedom, the assumption of management's powers by labor, and many other developments that may, or may not, be germane to the central issue of what has been happening to the way in which management performs its work and the effect of recent changes on the efficiency of the economy and the welfare of the society. History may help to clarify the central issues.

Some Basic Assumptions

The growth of industrial capitalism, at least in the Western world, was early seen as depending on the growth of capital. Hence many radical changes in the institutional structure were accepted in the expectation that they would contribute to the growth of capital and to its more efficient use. Correspondingly, many other proposals for change were shunted aside because of the deterrent effect that they might have on the accumulation of capital. The core of Adam Smith's theory was the proposition that economic growth could best be encouraged by granting every member of the body economic, and particularly the entrepreneur, a maximum degree of freedom to decide what he wanted to do with his time and money. It was expected that in the competition that would take place between individuals striving to get the most for what they had to sell and others seeking to buy as cheaply as possible, results would redound to the benefit of all—resources would be distributed in accordance with social priorities as reflected in the changing prices of the market place. And employers could be relied upon to strive constantly to improve their utilization of resources, for their efficiency was the key to the profits they would be able to earn.

This is not the place to trace, in detail, how the doctrine of laissez-faire won the day. The story has been told in one of our early studies. But it may help to set in perspective the current discussion of management's prerogatives if we recall some of the historical landmarks. The new doctrine of economic freedom had scarcely been ensconced in England as the cornerstone of public policy early in the nineteenth century before it was subjected to an attack on two fronts: the conservative landowners, incensed with the degradation of the laboring masses incident to the establishment of the factory system, passed protective legislation relating particularly to the maximum hours of labor and other basic conditions of work. And various groups of workers, having discovered that their newly expanded freedom was a passport to misery rather than to prosperity, sought to alter the basis on which they sold their labor. By joining together into a trade union, they hoped to force the employer to grant higher wages and better working conditions than they could possibly extract if they continued to approach him as individuals.

These earliest efforts to restrict the power of the entrepreneur met with intense opposition from the business community. Leading businessmen had recourse to first principles. They contended that an attack on their freedom of decision-making was an attack on freedom itself. If a man could arbitrarily be deprived of the value of his property by the action of the legislature or through the actions of a conspiracy among workers, then no man's freedom would be secure for long. They argued that in reducing the number of hours of labor from thirteen to twelve, Parliament was well on the way to killing the hen that laid the golden egg. They insisted that their profits came from the last hour of work and that in eliminating it, Parliament placed their profits in jeopardy. And profits were the foundation for an expanding capitalism. Without profits, there could be no capital accumulation; and, without capital accumulation, there could be no economic progress.

The employers' response was quick and sharp. Many argued that untrammelled competition was essential, for their very existence and survival depended on their driving as hard a bargain as possible. Karl Marx sought to demonstrate "scientifically" that the inexorable laws of capitalism left the employer no option but to squeeze the maximum amount of work out of his employees while paying them as little as possible, for only through extracting surplus value from his employees could he insure his own survival. Other critics of the new industrialism placed the responsibility for human exploitation on the cupidity of the businessman rather than on the impersonal logic of the market place. They saw in the employer's intransigent attitudes towards government, labor, and all others who sought to mitigate the harshness of the competitive system a ruthless drive for power and profits, without care or consideration for the human costs.

But there is another way of looking at the reaction that swept through the employer group when it began to be harried, however slightly, by a government considerate of labor and an embryonic trade union movement. Capitalistic enterprise is permeated with risk. While it holds out promise of large profits to the successful, the unsuccessful stand to lose their capital and their business. There are many factors that can upset even a successful enterprise. A sudden shift in demand can wipe out a lucrative market. A sudden fall in prices can turn prospective profits into sizeable losses. A new invention can cancel the special advantages that a concern has long enjoyed. A bad investment can lead to a long term competitive disadvantage. A new law may open a hitherto protected market to competitors. The businessman is never sure what the morrow will bring. But of this he can be certain; he must be in a position to respond to new conditions quickly and surely. Otherwise he will lose out to his competitors.

Living in a world characterized by constant and large-scale changes from which he cannot immunize himself, the only hope that the businessman has for success and growth is to develop high orders of foresight and flexibility. He must make his plans in light of changes which may occur, and he must retain as much flexibility as possible so as to be able to adjust rapidly to those changes which he could not initially foresee.

Small wonder, therefore, that the captain of industry, from the early days of industrial capitalism right down to today, has been genuinely concerned and disturbed about any and all attempts to reduce his freedom of action in reaching decisions about the use of the resources under his control.

The larger the number of uncontrolled forces affecting his ability to make a profit, the more intent he will be to protect his freedom of action in areas where he can influence the outcome. In earlier decades, wages accounted for by far the largest component of the manufacturer's cost. They were the crux to his flexibility. His ability to respond quickly and surely to the vagaries of the market, both domestic and international, depended on protecting his freedom of action to alter the number, utilization, and wages of his work force. If prices began to slip, the best chance of maintaining his competitive position was to lower the selling price—and he could do this only if he were in a position to institute changes that would result in lowering his costs, particularly his labor costs. If a new and much improved process was introduced by competitors which enabled them to cut their costs and prices and improve their product, his survival might depend on how quickly he could introduce the same or similar machinery and make corresponding improvements which could be reflected in lower prices. In order to survive in the rough and tumble of the competitive system, the employer had to stay in command of his enterprise, constantly on the alert to exploit new opportunities and equally on the alert to beat back new challenges. It was a grueling and exhausting undertaking but it offered substantial rewards to the successful just as it gave no quarter to the indolent or the stupid.

At least this was the simplified picture of the competitive economy developed by the economists and others who were enamoured of the benefits of an expanding industrialization. There was enough basis in reality for this doctrine to become firmly entrenched but the critics had no difficulty in pointing to the wide gap between the theory and the facts.

Limitations on Business Freedom

Despite the great value that businessmen attached to protecting their freedom of decision-making, the inherent instability of the competitive market was so great that they themselves sought relief from some of the pressures by developing sufficient power to repeal the "laws" of supply and demand, by entering into arrangements with fellow businessmen to restrict and restrain the intensity with which they would compete, and by seeking the assistance of government.

From government, businessmen frequently sought protection against competition from abroad, assistance in securing or maintaining special privileges abroad; special support in the form of grants of capital, subsidies, credit, tax remissions, and a wide variety of other special benefits. Few businessmen recognized any incongruity between their strong advocacy of a philosophy of laissez-faire and their equally strong efforts to secure favors from the government. The reconciliation came easily; any action that furthered the growth of business was in the public interest.

Hand in hand with the selective approach to government have been the efforts of businessmen to reach agreements, overtly and covertly, with other members of their industry to moderate the competitive struggle in the hope that a live and let live policy would provide sufficient opportunities for profit and gain while protecting the members of the group from the consequences of a sanguinary battle for supremacy in the market which could easily lead to the impoverishment of all.

The popular interpretation of the changing relations of government to business during the past many decades holds that the freedom of action of the entrepreneur to determine how he employs his capital and other resources, including his labor, has been successively reduced by the interference of government as it has sought to modify the untoward effects of competition on the more vulnerable members of the community. While there is considerable truth to this interpretation, it fails to take adequate note of the continuing efforts of the business community itself to escape from some of the more intense pressures of the competitive market.

There was nothing rational or normal about an economic order based on laissez-faire. England actually backed into the free market as it found the long-established system of state controls increasingly inadequate in a period of rapid technological and economic changes. And, even before the market became fully unfettered with the adoption of free trade in 1848, Parliament had already passed legislation to restrict and restrain the powers of businessmen.

In the United States, the business community never entertained the idea of operating completely without governmental assistance. The task of developing the country was too great for private capital to do it alone. When it suited their needs, as it often did, businessmen had no hesitancy whatever to seek special favors. But, when government sought to limit their power, they argued that such government action was a violation of their natural and constitutional rights. They went even further and argued that it was a violation of natural law for government to seek to protect the workingman and working-woman because such protection interfered with their basic freedom to sell their labor at any price which they might see fit.

While both England and the United States experienced rapid economic growth under an arrangement which reserved to the businessman a very wide area for decision-making, both government and business, for different reasons, found it desirable, in fact necessary, to modify, limit, and restrict the scope of freedom for entrepreneurial decision-making. The right of management to manage was never quite as absolute and unequivocal as many now believe.

The Transformation of Free Enterprise

As long as the owner of property and the manager was one and the same person and as long as there were many independent entrepreneurs, there were strong grounds for arguing, as did the fathers of this country, that a virile political democracy and economic freedom were mutually dependent. In a society of small landowners, small tradesmen, and independent artisans, each man controlled sufficient wealth or skill to yield him sufficient income to be economically secure, and, in turn, such economically independent persons eould be relied upon to protect their basic freedom by limiting the powers they assigned to and permitted the government to exercise on their behalf.

The prototype of a free enterprise system, based on competition among yeoman farmers and small tradesmen, had less and less relevance for the industrial structure that took shape towards the end of the nineteenth century, when the large trusts were beginning to dominate many key sectors of the American economy. But the transformation of the economy did not stop most advocates of market capitalism from seeking to justify the power concentration by reference to the first principle of the free enterprise system—the right of the owner of property, or his representatives, to decide on its use; and the advantage that accrued to a democratic society when the owners of property had the widest possible latitude in decision-making. For history was proof, if proof were required, of the beneficent effects of a competitive system which was the mainspring of the nation's rapid economic development and the marked gains in the individual's material well-being. But recourse to fundamentals could not indefinitely obscure or hide the increasing disparity between the terms of modern industrial life and the idealized preconditions of a competitive society composed of independent farmers, tradesmen, and artisans.

As the differences between folklore and fact mounted, a new tack was taken to derive and legitimize the prerogatives of management. Less and less was heard of rights and more and more was heard of functions for the American economy had become increasingly specialized. The day had passed when the individual businessman put up the capital, worked alongside his hired hands, and was responsible for every decision from the purchase of raw materials to the selling of the finished product. But many argued that the transformation in the terms of economic life were accompanied by transformations in the value and behavior of the leaders of the business community. Although the latter were, for the most part, managers rather than owners, they developed a high commitment to the corporation which employed them and were deeply concerned to realize all of its latent potentialities. The situation had changed but the goals remained the same: an expanding market and high profits.

The modern large corporation is a very intricate and complex institution which can operate effectively only if considerable skill is exercised to attract a wide range of resources and to utilize them effectively. The intricate structure of the modern corporation is suggested by the fact that among its senior officials there are likely to be vice-presidents for production, merchandizing, research and development, long-range planning, government contracts, international operations, finance, personnel, public relations, administration, and several more. The work force may number 100,000 or more—the American Telephone and Telegraph system has almost one million employees—and it may operate dozens or even hundreds of plants located in the United States and abroad.

These few reminders of the complex elements that go to make up the structure of the modern large corporation should suffice to establish the simple and incontrovertible fact that contemporary corporate enterprise is predicated on the efficient exercise of the managerial function. Clearly, some person, or group of persons, must be charged with the responsibility for planning, directing, and controlling the use of such a wide range of economic resources. There must be a fulcrum for decision-making. Large organizations cannot run themselves—although they frequently convey the impression that they do.

The Management Function

The explicit recognition of the management function has come slowly. The early economists barely recognized it. They simply assumed that it was in harmony with nature, democracy, and the pursuit of efficiency for the owners of capital and their representatives to have maximum freedom in determining how to use their resources. The economists limited their analysis to three basic elements—land, labor, and capital. Managerial skill, to the extent that they dealt with it at all, was subsumed under capital. The capitalist was entitled to a return on the money which he advanced as well as on the time and effort which he expended in directing its use. Writing at the turn of this century, the great Cambridge economist, Alfred Marshall, was more aware than his predecessors of managerial skill as a distinct resource but he did not integrate this new factor fully into his analytical framework.

Explicit recognition of the managerial function actually came about as a result of a series of largely unrelated developments. Prior to World War I, Frederick Taylor and his confreres laid the groundwork for the systematic application of engineering logic to the work place and demonstrated that important reductions in costs and gains in profits would follow upon the adoption of a scientific approach to management. Developments in dynamic psychology during the 1920s and 1930s prepared the ground for organizational efforts focused on altering the working environment with an aim of adding to the productivity of the work force. A new axis for employer action had been uncovered.

But it was the facts of life—although the facts came to be recognized very slowly—that forced the issue to the fore. Adam Smith had pointed to the implications of a split between owners and managers in his analysis of the great foreign trading corporations of his day. Many years later, Max Weber, the great German sociologist, had adumbrated the consequences of bureaucracy in modern life. But it was the popularizing work of Ripley of Harvard and Berle of Columbia, buttressed by statistical evidence, that finally made an impact on the American intellectual world at the time of the New Era and the Great Depression. The simple facts were these: large corporations were being run not by owners but by managers. While it was possible to derive the authority of the managers from that of the owners on whose behalf they exercised it, an alternative and perhaps even more realistic approach would find it grounded in the functions which they performed.

In the decade or so prior to the outbreak of World War II, a strenuous if limited effort was made to fashion a managerial ideology in the United States through the work of Elton Mayo and his collaborators at Harvard and of businessmen such as Chester Barnard who was more academic than the professors. Mayo and his colleagues stressed the unique role of the manager in eliciting and directing the human effort of the employees of a large corporation in a manner that would harmonize their personal needs with the goals of the company. Barnard was more concerned with analyzing the elasticity and constraints available to the managers of large organizations as they sought to realize the purposes of the enterprise.

But it was the exposure of many businessmen to the military command structure during World War II that did so much to accelerate the preoccupation with systematic management. The past decade and a half witnessed attempts by both captains of industry and professors of management to develop a more explicit rationale for the role of the corporate manager—and for the sources of his authority and the nature of his responsibility.

The high level of business activity and the sustained high profits during the past two decades at one and the same time appeared to establish proof of the effectiveness with which management was performing its essential functions and permitted and encouraged management to adopt a more experimental approach to the exercise of these functions. While management was under pressure to bargain with labor about a great many aspects of employment which it had previously considered exclusively within its own province, it did not hesitate to seek and receive government assistance in moderating such pressures, as through the passage of restrictive legislation which placed new obstacles in the path of unions.

Similarly, it broadened the definition of its basic function and advanced the doctrine that its responsibility was no longer limited to earning profits for the shareholders but encompassed adjudicating the competing claims of the owners, employees, customers, suppliers, and the community. Indicative of management's broadened approach was its claim, which it tested and had sustained in the courts, that it has the right to withhold some of the company's earnings in order to distribute them to worthy philanthropic causes.

But, at the same time, management, finding itself in a more exposed position and subject to pressure from an increasingly large number of special interest groups, broadened the scope of its functions. It succeeded in making itself increasingly an independent force and intensified its efforts to protect its flanks by pursuing an aggressive program aimed at influencing the opinion makers and educating the larger public in the fundamentals of the private enterprise system and the contemporary version of the large corporation, operated by a professional management for the benefit of all.

As management became increasingly self-conscious about its

responsibilities and duties, at least as reflected in its rhetoric, it also looked anew at its power and authority. It had long been aware that a democratic government was restricting the scope of its freedom, not so much as a punitive measure but as the inevitable concomitant of government's efforts to enlarge the range and quality of services that it rendered to the public and as it sought to fulfill the aspirations of the disadvantaged. Management suddenly became aware of a new threat on its labor flank. While it had long been accustomed to hard fights with labor about the division of the gains, it discovered that the cumulative results of collective bargaining were slowly shifting the line of demarcation between its own authority and that of the union. At this point, it raised the question whether it may not inadvertently have been party to the erosion of its own authority. With this recognition, it started a counter offensive. In 1960, the minority leader of the Senate, Dirksen of Illinois, reacting to a decision of the Supreme Court which interdicted the courts interfering with the arbitration process, introduced a bill to "amend the Norris-La Guardia Act and other Labor laws." The National Association of Manufacturers' (NAM) commentary on this bill stated that it "proposes to assist in restoring the function of managing a business to the management where the responsibility rests and the function and authority belong." The NAM went on to say that the responsibilities and functions of management in conducting a business with proper foresight and planning are very broad—including, among other responsibilities, the determination of products; the location, relocation, and closing of units; the layout and equipment to be used; the determination of financial and pricing policies; the determination of job contract, including the duties to be performed in any given job, determining the size of the work force, the allocation and assignment of work, the determination of policies affecting the selection and promotion of employees, the establishment of quality standards, the scheduling of operations, and the number of shifts required.

The NAM concluded: "Over a period of years all of the areas in this partial list of management responsibilities and functions have been encroached upon by labor organizations seeking to control the operations of employers. As the sponsor of the present proposal has indicated, legislation embodying the principles of this bill is essential if our free enterprise system is to continue to operate and to utilize technological improvements as a means of progress towards a higher standard of living for all."

The Supreme Court, with only a single dissenter, has recently adumbrated the doctrine that "strictly a function of management" must be interpreted as referring only to that over which the contract gives management "complete control and unfettered discretion." No reference is made to the rights of property or even to the basic authority essential for the effective discharge of managerial responsibility. What management can or cannot do is made to depend, in the terms of the highest court of the land, on agreements reached with representatives of the workers and on the interpretations growing out of these agreements by those elected by the parties to review the evidence and render a decision.

This, indeed, points to a major turning in the road.

3. The Goals of Workers

For two thousand years and more, religious leaders have preached the doctrine of human dignity and respect for the individual but their preachings and teachings in this regard went largely unheeded because, among other reasons, the struggle for survival was so intense. Most men had to struggle from sunup to sundown to earn enough to feed their families and themselves. In time of war or national calamity, many were unable to secure even the minimum required for survival and died a speedy or a slow death.

Only those who were able to command the labor of others could escape from the treadmill of incessant work and grinding poverty. Since men had never willingly parted with the fruits of their labor, it usually required the exercise of power to effect such transfers from the hapless many to the fortunate few. In the recent senatorial campaign in Massachusetts, a worker challenged Mr. Ted Kennedy during a factory tour with the statement, "I understand you've never worked a day in your life," and, while the startled candidate mumbled an inaudible reply, the worker added, "Well, let me tell you, you haven't missed a thing."

While the margins above mere subsistence increased in Western Europe in the two centuries before the French Revolution as a result of the extension of the market and the improvements in technology, political freedom and economic well-being were still restricted to a small minority. The vast majority, in England as well as on the continent, had neither.

Without a vision of a better future, men must reconcile themselves to the realities of the present, no matter how dreary, deadly, and dangerous these realities may be. In the face of overwhelming power, they have even reconciled themselves to the galley and the concentration camp.

The American and French revolutions provided the vision of a better future, not for the few, or even the many—but for all. These revolutions held forth a promise of freedom for the individual. No longer would man be subject at worst to the pleasure or the whim of authority, or, at best, to the *noblesse oblige* of the king or viceroy. Henceforth, they themselves would be party to deciding on the limitations of their own freedom.

While the elimination of arbitrary political power is a necessary condition for the establishment of freedom, it is not sufficient to assure freedom. For if men must barter themselves or their wives and children in order to secure the essentials for living or if they must barter their labor during most of their waking hours in order to acquire these essentials, their freedom is severely limited. They can enjoy it mostly when they sleep.

The English laboring man in the early days of industrial capitalism had a considerable number of rights and privileges— many more than had workers in other countries. But he was not a full-fledged citizen who participated directly in the political process. He had no direct part in determining the laws and regulations that governed his life and work. And, at the very time that government began to remove its heavy hand, he found that another weighed increasingly upon him.

Forced to barter his labor for a wage, he found himself for twelve hours of the day under the authority of his employer. Since more people were looking for jobs than there were jobs available, he not only had to agree to whatever wage his employer was willing to pay him but he had to endure chastisements and fines for breaches of rules of conduct and discipline.

Moreover, he had to strain his body and muscles to match the pace of the employer's machines; he could not absent himself from the bench—even to take care of his urgent needs—without the permission of his supervisor. And, in all ways, large and small, he was, in Marx's terminology, an industrial slave who might at any moment be discharged, no matter how long or how faithfully he had worked.

There was a gap between the revolutionary promises of a better life for all and the stark realities of the laboring man's existence. His only chance of making the promise come true, short of working towards the destruction of his society through revolution, was to exert pressure on two fronts—the political and the industrial—in the hope that he could eventually secure a major voice in determining the conditions governing the way in which he lived and worked.

There was an important difference, as well as many similarities, in the struggles of British and American workers. The former found it much more difficult to establish their rights to full citizenship. It was not until the latter years of the nineteenth century that the British worker without property was permitted to vote. Even more important was the much harder struggle engaged in by the British worker before he was recognized as an individual entitled to be treated with personal dignity—irrespective of his social origin, uncouth speech, and limited education. In a class-conscious society, every man is not as good as every other; just the opposite. The best men were those who belonged to the upper classes. And workingmen were at the bottom of the ladder.

The American constitution had laid the groundwork for the

full-fledged political freedom for all except the slave population. Free land and relative shortages of labor enabled most Americans to escape from the extreme economic duress that characterized the British worker during the early decades of industrialization. Since this nation did not have a true aristocracy of blood, status, or wealth, the American with limited means might be pitied but not despised. For many of the leaders of society had only recently left poverty behind.

But important as those initial differences were—and they left their mark on all that has transpired since—by the turn of this century, there were many striking parallels between the two countries. The working population in both countries had the right to vote but the prevailing ethos in both societies was to limit the role of government in the operation of the economy. Labor, through its unions, had succeeded in exerting more pressure on employers, but the balance of power remained very much with the owners of capital.

There were small groups of workers in England and the United States who argued that the long-delayed realization of a better day for the mass of mankind could be achieved only through the overturn of the capitalistic system. The mass of British labor looked forward, however, to substantial but less radical reforms in the ownership structure. American labor, in contrast, openly professed its support for the system of free enterprise. It wanted changes but these changes related to the way in which the system functioned—not to its basic structure and objectives. Gompers' statement is relevant. When asked what American labor wanted, he said, "More, more, more." He also insisted that the more unforgivable crime that a businessman could commit was to fail to make a profit.

Most people assumed, and quite correctly, that Gompers's "more" referred to wages. But they did not appreciate—and

Gompers himself may have been unclear about the matter—
that the workers wanted not only more wages but also more of
all the desirable things of life: more job security, more leisure,
more freedom from the employer's arbitrary actions, more opportunity to be trained and promoted, more protection in their
old age, more assurance that their skill and training would not
be made obsolescent by the installation of a new machine, more
freedom to speak their minds both on and off the job, more consideration by the employer for their health and safety, more rest
periods, more equitable work schedules, more vacations—in
fact, and this was most significant, the list was without end for
as opportunity offered, new objectives could be added. While
the economists of an earlier day were undoubtedly right in arguing that man's desires were unlimited, it was a vulgar error on
their part, and on the part of all those who subscribed to their
doctrine, to see these desires solely in terms of material goods.
Men will not fight, much less die, for a second suit of clothes
or even for a second car.

Recognizing that there was little likelihood of obtaining the
good things in life, material and otherwise, through the inter-
vention of government since the mood of the country precluded
the government's interfering directly with regard to the conditions under which people worked or the rewards which they
received, the nascent trade union movement pragmatically addressed itself to the task of strengthening its bargaining power
to secure its most important objectives from the employer. It
had no alternative.

The major thrust of labor's effort was directed towards achiev-
ing a trinity composed of organization, higher wages, and job
security. Organization was by far the most important of the
three for once achieved, it would provide the fulcrum with
which to force the employer to bargain with the union about

the terms of employment. No longer would he be in a position
to determine unilaterally—subject only to the pressures of the
competitive market—what he would pay, whom he would hire,
whom he would promote, whom he would discharge, how fast
he would operate his machines, whether he would install safety
devises—and the myriad of other decisions important to him
because of their effect on his costs and therefore on his competitive position; and important to the men and women who
worked for him because these factors determined to such a large
extent the quality of their lives, on and off the job.

Although American labor leaders repeatedly testified before
Congressional committees and other public bodies that they
staunchly supported the capitalistic system, they saw no incongruity in pressing the employer group as hard as possible for improvements in wages, hours, and working conditions. Labor's
admiration for the competitive system never went so far as to
inhibit it from pressing its claims for more. The workers heard
spokesmen for capitalism argue that no worthwhile and surely
no permanent gains could be achieved except through the
mechanism of the free market, but they were not impressed by
these contentions.

The same employers who beat a direct path to Congress for
tariff protection argued that it was impossible for them to grant
their workers higher wages because they were already paying
very much more than employers overseas. Trade unionists challenged this contention because, despite the fact that the United
States had always had a level of wages far above that prevailing in other countries, American businessmen were usually able
to make large profits. The relation between the wages that employers paid, their labor costs, and their profits was much less
direct than the conservative interpreters of capitalism pre-
tended. Since the domestic market was protected from foreign

competition by the costs of transportation and a tariff wall, and since exports accounted for only a small percent of total sales, American labor concluded early that it had little to lose if wages were raised. Trade union efforts would have to be very successful indeed before they could jeopardize the future of the enterprises for which their members worked. Here was still another fundamental difference between American and British labor, for the latter learned early from the dependence of Great Britain on foreign trade that their wages did have a direct bearing on the competitive position of the enterprise for which they worked and therefore on the future of their own jobs.

Despite its pragmatic objectives, American labor found it difficult to organize and to press its claims. A major obstacle to labor's efforts was the fact that employers could usually count on the might of government and the law. There were additional deterrents such as the constant inflow of the large number of immigrants who were willing to take whatever jobs were available, even if the conditions were hazardous and the wages low. In addition, of course, the ablest people—those who might otherwise have risen to positions of leadership—left the ranks of labor as opportunities opened up. Nevertheless, despite these and other difficulties, labor made substantial strides in organizing the crafts as well as other sectors of the industrial economy— such as mining, clothing, and railroading—where the pattern of work or the characteristics of the workers, or both, established a predisposition toward trade unions.

The establishment of a union implies not only that employers and employees must develop mechanisms for adjusting their differences but also that the union must strive for the establishment of rules and regulations that will allocate equitably the available jobs among its members, for a union is a voluntary organization whose strength depends in the first instance on the loyalty and support of its members. And the overriding interest of the union member is his job, particularly in holding it as he grows older and his strength and vitality begin to diminish.

The struggle between the generations is characteristic of all peoples at all times but the American labor market at the turn of this century was unique in that the numbers of its young people were being swelled by the large-scale inflow from abroad. Small wonder, therefore, that American trade unions placed major stress on seniority which alone could protect the older worker. In fact, the impetus to the establishment of craft unions was to protect a group of established workers against competition from newcomers.

Seniority—an orderly system of advancement, layoff, and recall based on length of service—is not an easy policy to establish and maintain. Employers will almost always fight its introduction because it restricts their ability to hire, promote, and fire. They fear that a seniority system will force them to favor the less capable man with the result that their labor costs will rise. Some of their fears are justified but the continued profitability of many concerns with strong seniority is presumptive evidence that employers' fears have often been exaggerated. What is more, a seniority system frequently prevents many troublesome personnel issues from arising.

But the establishment of a seniority system is a beginning, not an end. The system cannot be self-operating. Through contract and arbitration, answers must be found as to the unit within which seniority prevails; the conditions under which the employer is permitted to disregard seniority in selecting workers for training or promotion; whether seniority with respect to layoff or discharge must follow exactly the same pattern as in the case of recall or the allocation of overtime. How are seniority rights handled when a particular unit is discontinued and its work is parcelled out among other units? What happens when a man selected for supervision fails to make the grade and returns to the bench? Or when another, who made the grade and served as a supervisor for a decade or more, finds that his position is eliminated and he must return to worker status? If the job is crucial to the worker, then these questions and many more like them assume an urgency and importance that transcends all other facets of the employment relation. It was in this arena that American trade unions early made a significant contribution to their members. In the decades before the establishment of private pension systems and social security benefits, seniority was the worker's basic security; and, even today, it continues to have the most pronounced and direct influence on his employment status.

Unions have failed to attract large numbers of white collar and women workers mainly because these groups have less concern with seniority. White collar employment has been much more stable than blue collar, and the majority of women workers have tended to move in and out of the labor market. The efforts of the trade union movement to organize these groups will probably continue to be particularly difficult unless the attachment of women to the labor market becomes more regular or white collar employment becomes more unstable. Both are likely to occur and may already be under way.

The slow but steady growth of American trade unions after the early years of the century was accelerated by the tight labor market of World War I, but organized labor lost some of its position during the "New Era" when manufacturing employment grew slowly; industrialists pursued elaborate welfare policies to thwart the growth of unions; and the mood of the country was reflected in the successive elections of Harding, Coolidge, and Hoover with their pronounced bias in favor of big business, small government, and their conservative attitudes toward the expansion of human rights.

The Great Depression of 1929–1933, which brought the economy to the verge of collapse and the society to the brink of upheaval, left an indelible mark on American labor. In the absence of jobs, seniority had little value. The depression proved beyond a shadow of a doubt that the employer could not assure the workingman a job. And so labor, which had for so long put most of its energies into extracting gains from the employer group, shifted its attention increasingly to seeking benefits from government. And, in the years that followed, it got much from government: assistance in organizing, friendly tribunals before which to plead its cases of conflict with employers, unemployment insurance, and old age and survivors' benefits—and much more. It had a new opportunity to fill out its ranks, regroup, and reenter the fray of bargaining with the employer in a much strengthened position.

The spectacular recovery of the economy as a result of World War II pushed wages up very rapidly but it also laid the basis for certain additional labor gains. As the war progressed it became public policy to try to hold the line on wages and prices; as a result the War Labor Board looked with favor on agreements between management and labor that stressed deferred benefits, such as the employer's payment of premiums for health and hospital insurance, vacations with pay, additional holidays, pensions. Moreover, management and labor agreed to many new work rules which had the double-barrelled objective of speeding output and at the same time increasing the earnings of labor.

The level of the economy since the end of World War II contributed to further improvement in the welfare of the laboring population: average weekly earnings in manufacturing rose in 1962 to over $97. (in contrast to about $25. at the beginning of World War II). Even after allowing for inflation and higher taxes, the real disposable income of a married worker with three dependents increased by more than one-half during this period. And, currently, most workers are employed in establishments where both office and plant personnel receive 7 or 8 paid holidays in the year; up to 3 weeks paid vacations; and where they have life insurance, hospital insurance, surgical and medical insurance, sickness and accident insurance, and retirement pensions. Moreover, the basic work week has been reduced to forty hours or less.

In recent years, labor has found that the employer is once again a good source of additional gains. His profits have been sufficiently high and sufficiently sustained to enable him to agree to many substantial improvements in the employment contract. Many students have questioned the basis for these managerial concessions for they believe that when business agrees to a wage increase it turns right around and raises prices, thereby establishing the circuit for a continuing inflation. There has even been some uneasiness in the ranks of labor that this may be the case and that what workers gain in higher wages they lose in higher prices. But, in the face of high profits, no labor leader could long survive if he did not succeed in getting more for his members. There is much more basic democracy in unions than most critics realize. This is not to say either that there are no differences in objectives between trade union management and the members nor that all trade unions are operated solely for the benefit of the members. One need not stretch the analogy very far to recognize that not all businesses are run for the benefit of stockholders.

But, again, union members are interested in much more than

their wage rate. They want more money now but they also want more money in the future—when they are sick, or unemployed, or retired. The several governmental programs are good but they are not good enough. Hence, the renewed pressure on the employer. Too few business leaders have understood the necessity of determining whether it is better from their point of view to have industry or the community carry the cost of new social benefits. Management must sensibly anticipate that labor will be successful in an expanding economy in improving its rewards. The only issue is the locus of such gains. Here, management has scope for influencing the outcome. Management cannot successfully oppose improving the state unemployment system without running the risk of having a strong union bargain successfully for supplementary unemployment benefits. After pensions were introduced in the steel industry, management lobbied for a rise in social security benefits.

A new trend appears on the horizon. The combined value of unemployment insurance and supplementary unemployment benefits are resulting in some unions considering clauses which would give the worker with seniority the right to first layoff. More broadly, the worker is concerned about what the contract affords him when wages and leisure are both kept in purview.

Workers also want more leisure. They want to work less so that they will have more opportunity to enjoy the good things which their higher wages have now brought within their scope. But they have also begun to advocate a further reduction in the work week because they are restive about the signs which indicate what the acceleration in technological change may do to their jobs. They know about the serious redundancy of labor in mining, steel, automobiles, meat packing, and other sectors. Over the years, the gains in productivity have been divided into about three-fifths in the form of more goods and two-fifths in the form of more leisure. With vastly more emphasis now than previously on research and development, the threat to jobs from technological advances is much greater and labor has consequently begun to press for a shorter work week.

Over the years, then, the American worker has been able to improve substantially the quality of his life off the job by virtue of the reduction in hours and increases in wages which he has been able to obtain, plus a considerable number of fringe benefits. All of these gains, he has secured from his employer. In addition, he has secured important gains from government that have helped to raise his standard of living.

The substantial and continuing gains that he has made and that have been enhanced in many families by the fact that his wife is also a wage earner, have tended to shift his focus increasingly to the conditions under which he works—the eight hours or so that he spends every day, five days a week, in earning the money which enables him to support his family.

The conditions under which he works have also vastly improved; no longer is he exposed to dangerous machinery or to health hazards; no longer is he exhausted at the end of the day so that all that he wants is to find oblivion in drink or in sleep; no longer is he bullied by the foreman. Despite these and other substantial gains, he is not satisfied. From the time he enters the plant until the quitting whistle, he is not in control of himself. His body, his mind, even his soul belong in some degree to those who are paying him. He is under their authority. They tell him what to do and what not to do. They even tell him how to do it. They set the pace and determine the rest periods. In fact, almost every decision of importance has been made by others who supervise him.

This subordination is not a condition of servitude because

he is free to get up and leave. But how free is he when his major option is to enter upon a similar arrangement with another employer who will exercise the same order of authority and control over him?

It does not follow necessarily from the fact that American workers today have much better work conditions than did employees at the turn of the century that their feelings reflect those objective facts. For feelings are determined only in part by reality. They also depend on more subjective considerations. Even on the objective side, one trend has been adverse. Advances in technology and in the theory and practice of management have led to a much tighter scheduling of work and a much more elaborate system of articulating the work of different groups. The result has been more and tighter supervision, or at least more dependence of workers on the flow of work set by others. The new technology may be reversing this trend. The more rapid increase in non-production jobs is operating to make tight controls much more difficult.

But what of the man himself? How has he changed? A significant proportion of the industrial work force early in the century were immigrants or the children of immigrants. Most of these immigrants came from countries where power and property had long been concentrated in the hands of the few. They had known neither freedom nor comfort. They had emigrated to the United States either because they had no option or because they looked forward to making a better life for themselves and their children in the New World. These people were used to very little, expected very little, and were satisfied with very little—at least, until they learned that many others had much more and that they too, with work and luck, might achieve much more.

The American worker today is likely to be native-born; in fact, most American workers had grandparents who were born here. During his formative years, the worker is indoctrinated with ideas of equality and freedom—with the belief that every man is as good as every other man. Further, he is taught that all distinctions based on education, wealth, family, or other social criteria have little importance, since a man should be judged by what he does, not by his parents or by the schools which he attends.

And he knows that three times within three decades his father and he were called to arms to make secure the freedom and liberties which give meaning to the American dream.

Nurtured on this heady drink of freedom and equality, of liberty and justice, he cannot fail to become restive, disturbed, antagonistic by what he finds in the employment situation. From the moment the starting whistle blows, his freedom is in suspense; justice is in jeopardy; one man is clearly the superior of another; power and authority permeate the work place.

Philosophers and lawyers earn their livelihood by making distinctions, refined and subtle. They can explain to their own satisfaction and to the satisfaction of the owners of capital and their representatives who manage their enterprises for them that there is no contradiction between the practice of democracy in the political arena and the presence of autocracy in the world of work.

The average man is neither philosopher nor lawyer, but he is a man who sees his life as a whole. He cannot live without tension by one set of values in the hours during which he works and live by an entirely different set of values during the hours when he is off the job.

The lessons of democracy which have been drilled into him tend to become the touchstone for all of his actions. Experience has taught him that he need no longer fear for bread; in fact, he can afford cake. Much of what he has struggled for, he has gained.

But, in the arena of work itself where he spends so much of life and energy, he is mocked. Small wonder, therefore, that it is here that he is seeking to realize the democratic values which he holds dear.

PART TWO
MANAGERIAL IMPERATIVES

4. Economics of Location and Specialization

The motive power of the capitalistic system is the entrepreneur's search for situations which hold promise of yielding large profits. Of only slightly lesser importance is the effort that entrepreneurs must make to protect investments which they have made in the past. It is inherent in capitalistic enterprise that no entrepreneur, no matter how advantageous his present position, is ever secure against the disturbances that time and change can bring in their wake.

The ownership of property implies the right to dispose of it in any manner the owner sees fit, subject only to the rights of others that have standing in the law. For example, a man usually cannot cut his wife out of his will, for the law insists that she has a claim to a part of his wealth.

Over the years, the law has likewise come to interdict the owner of property from using it for the explicit purpose of injuring others. Hence, large firms cannot directly seek to destroy small ones. The law also has something to say about what the owners of property may or may not do if, in the exercise of their rights, they lower the value of other property or harm the community. An entrepreneuer cannot buy the cheapest fuel if, in using it, he creates a noxious smoke nuisance that lessens the value of other people's property.

We call attention to these well-known limitations on the

freedom of action of the owner of property only to remind the reader that there are no absolute rights in our society, except the right of conscience. Tradition and law support a very wide scope of action for property owners, but limits do exist and these are subject to change with time—as a society reassesses the relative gains and losses which accrue from moving the boundary line between the area of individual initiative and social control.

The logic of the competitive system requires a high degree of initiative on the part of the entrepreneur to exploit and react to the opportunities and changes in the market. In classical economic theory profit is a reward for those who have exercised the greatest skill in combining the various factors of production. With costs lower than his competitors, the successful entrepreneur can enjoy a wider margin of profit. Entrepreneurial initiative, particularly entrepreneurial imagination and innovation, holds the key to profits and therefore to the success and survival of a business.

Among the most important dimensions of entrepreneurial initiative is the decision of the employer as to where to locate, or relocate, his plant. It was suggested, earlier, that one of the foundation stones of capitalistic enterprise is the free movement of capital, for only in that manner can initiative be stimulated and rewarded, and the consumer and the community be assured that gains in productivity will result in price reductions. Changes in the density of population, in the means of transportation, in the technology of manufacturing, and still others which are characteristic of a dynamic society and economy are constantly altering the margins of advantage and disadvantage which result from the location of plants. For example, the very rapid increase in the population of California in recent years has made it profitable for concerns to locate there whereas previously the smallness of the market proved to be a barrier to expansion.

Many communities in the South are now avidly seeking to broaden and deepen their industrial base. They offer a great number of special benefits to prospective employers—ranging all the way from a rent-free plant for a number of years to special tax reductions.

Much relocation occurs in response to advances in technology. Paper companies find that they can use southern pine where previously they could not. The opening up of a new natural gas field makes it highly advantageous to locate high power consuming plants nearby. A modern industrial economy is constantly in transformation as alert employers seek to take advantage of new markets for raw materials or new consumer markets in response to changes in demography, technology, income levels, and tax structures.

There runs through much of economic theory a conviction about the virtue of mobility for capital and labor alike. Students of the American experience have made much of the latter, pointing out that the willingness of men and women to respond to opportunity—even when, as in the settlement of the West, great physical danger lurked in the path—largely explains the speed of our economic development. Employers never have had to wait very long to get the workers they need to turn an opportunity into a reality—as long as they were willing to raise their wage offer high enough.

An optimum allocation of resources does not require all capital to be mobile, nor all workers to be willing to pull up stakes and move. The early economists had already recognized that money spent on plant and equipment was fixed and should be considered sunk. But capitalistic enterprise is an ongoing process and its successful operation requires freedom for new funds to flow to wherever the opportunities appear to be greatest. Likewise, it early came to be recognized that even if all artificial barriers to the movement of labor were removed—such as the old Settlement Acts which interfered with mobility in the England of Adam Smith—many among the working population would be loath to pick themselves up and relocate to areas where opportunities for employment and earnings would be greater. It was Smith himself who pointed out that of all baggage, man is the most difficult to transport.

In recent years, new dimensions of the mobility problem have come to the surface as scholars and the public have recognized that a system of private accounts—the advantages and disadvantages to a private employer—does not adequately portray the entire range of costs and benefits that may be involved. As long as the mobility of labor and capital were part and parcel of a process of economic expansion, the weight of the evidence appeared to be overwhelmingly in its favor, for the allocation of resources was apparently thereby improved. But, recently, serious questions are being raised about certain types of relocation. If, for example, the major reason for relocating a plant from the North to the South is to take advantage of special governmental benefits in the new locale and to escape from a northern trade union, the social balance sheet may not show a net gain. Such a balance sheet must take into consideration the reduction, if not destruction, of individual and communal property values in the older industrial area. And, as we shall see, the courts and arbitrators who confront these questions are concerned with still another issue. They are frequently pressed to weigh the costs involved in such relocations to particular groups of workers —especially those who have given long years of faithful service to an employer who now plans to abandon them.

The basic question is not whether management has the right to relocate but rather whether, in the presence of a collective agreement with a union, it can unilaterally decide to close down its operations, in whole or in part, and in the process jeopardize a whole bundle of rights that workers may have acquired as a result of years of service.

A related question arises with respect to the rights of management to determine unilaterally what to produce and sell in the hope and expectation of making a profit. What, indeed, is more integral to the managerial function than determining the range of products or services on which the enterprise should specialize. But, even after the entrepreneur has made his decision about what to produce, he still must decide what to buy and what to make on his own. Some large companies that aim at complete vertical integration are engaged in every stage of business—from securing the raw materials to marketing the finished products and even to consumer financing. Most entrepreneurs, however, specialize within a narrower band. For instance, they buy components and sell manufactured products to others who take over the distribution functions.

Even so, once a pattern is established, it does not necessarily remain fixed. One of the challenges that entrepreneurs face is whether to continue in, or to modify, their field of specialization. They may expand and start to manufacture new items rather than continue to buy goods or services from others. On the other hand, they may move in the opposite direction and discontinue the production of certain items because they believe that on balance they will increase their margin of profit if they start to buy these items. The continuing evaluation of their best position with respect to the range and depth of their specialization represents a central area for managerial decision-making.

Individuals who have not been directly involved in collective bargaining and arbitration may not see at first how any question can arise about the right of management to determine unilaterally whether to continue to produce or to contract out, that is, to purchase goods and services required for their manufacturing activities. It may be difficult to see the basis for a union's having a say in such a matter. One exception would be if management formally agreed, as part of a larger arrangement with a union, to restrict its right to contract out. Parties are always free to restrict their rights for considerations that they value more highly. The interesting and important point to note is that conflicts about contracting out have arisen increasingly in recent years even though management never agreed to any limitation on its right to do so; even in the face of a failure of the union to write such a provision into the agreement. The determination of an employer to change his pattern of production and to buy what he previously produced would appear to be a matter which lies properly within his discretion. However, let us explore some additional facets of the problem.

When a union signs a collective bargaining agreement with an employer, it is first and foremost participating in a complex of arrangements that will determine who will work, what they will receive in wages, and a large number of other conditions that bear on the security and welfare of the workingman. If the employer, having agreed to these stipulations, takes unilateral action to eliminate work which he has performed in the past, he may destroy, or seriously weaken, the bargaining unit with which he has negotiated. This kind of action is tantamount to a "breach of contract."

His move to subcontract may be nothing more or less than the seizing of a new opportunity to cut his costs and increase his profits. Or it may represent, for an employer who is in a tight position, the margin between breaking even or suffering a loss. The move to subcontract may have quite different effects on the work force. In one case, it may jeopardize the jobs of senior employees; in others, it may prevent the recall of workers with low seniority; in still others, it may represent nothing more than an unwillingness of the employer to proffer work to unskilled workers in the local labor market. There is no need to indicate the whole range of possibilities. Enough has been said to underline the point that what looked initially as an unquestioned right of management turns out to be intertwined with rights that labor has gained as a result of its contractual agreement.

At this point, it could be argued that the responsibility and the right of management is to manage and fundamental in this context are decisions where to locate and what to produce. If management is no longer free to make such decisions, then, indeed, the free enterprise system as we have known it is no more.

However, there have long been restraints on management's freedom of decision to locate and its freedom to determine the scope of its specialization. In fact, limitations of its freedom have resulted from actions taken by itself.

The extent to which entrepreneurs are able to specialize profitably in particular fields depends in no small measure on whether or not their costs are approximately equal to or below those of foreign producers after allowance has been made for freight and other market differentials. Since foreign producers frequently have a range of advantages which tend to lower their costs below those of even an efficient domestic employer, American industrialists have long sought and frequently obtained tariff protection or other relief. They have long sought the assistance of government to enhance the value of their property rights through special subsidies, tax considerations, and similar measures. While successful in a great many instances, they have been increasingly rebuffed of late in matters of the tariff, an arena that has long affected the right of management to specialize.

Public policy on the domestic front also has a significant effect on the allied consideration of location. In addition to the long established rights of local government to zone different parcels of land for different uses and therefore to prohibit the use of certain land for industrial purposes, the complicated system of freight rates has exercised a major influence on the pattern of industrial location and development. There is a considerable body of evidence which suggests that the southeast has long been handicapped in the attraction and expansion of industry because of an adverse rate structure. And, while the truck has helped to reduce some of these competitive disadvantages, the fact is that, to the extent that adverse railroad tariffs remain in effect, many industrialists who might otherwise prefer to locate in the South will not do so.

We see, then, that within the framework of this country's economic development and contemporary business environment, management's freedom to locate and specialize has never been absolute and that recently it is increasingly affected by considerations of national policy. The location of major defense industries, such as aircraft, is, of course, not only influenced by but also largely determined by government. Government is likewise influencing to a marked degree the type of items on which many contractors specialize. In addition, it frequently exercises marked leverage over many aspects of the work performed by prime contractors and subcontractors. A great diversity of other governmental programs bear directly on considerations of location, such as criteria for allocating government contracts to areas with high unemployment, and the specific Area Redevelopment efforts aimed at the rehabilitation of seriously depressed areas. In these and many other ways, the freedom of management to determine where to locate and what to produce is significantly influenced both by what government does and what it does not do.

With this background, we can now undertake an appraisal of the way in which the courts and arbitrators have dealt with management's right to determine its location and specialization when challenged by a trade union or a group of workers. No court or arbitrator is likely to be insensitive to considerations of costs, profitability, and the survival of the enterprise. But they may decide to broaden the scope of their inquiry to include an evaluation of the human costs, hitherto borne by the worker, or even social costs, hitherto borne by the community, in reaching a judgment as to the proper balance between efficiency and equity. If this is their approach, they know that they will not be the first, nor the last, to be involved in shifting the boundaries within which business enterprise operates. A summary review of the salient facts in selective cases and an evaluation of the reasoning of the arbitrators and the judges will help to shed light on the extent to which shifts are occurring in the rights of management in this area.

Location

In April, 1957, the Stetson Hat Company, which a decade earlier had acquired the Mallory Hat Company, decided to move its Mallory finishing shop from Danbury, Connecticut, to its Philadelphia plant. It had recently signed a three year agreement with the Danbury local which was a member of the same union that represented the workers in its Philadelphia shop. When apprised of the contemplated move, the Philadelphia local threatened a sympathy strike unless the company kept the entire Danbury plant operating until the expiration of the three year contract. This threat was made despite the company's offer of jobs in Philadelphia for those who would lose them in Danbury and severance pay for those who did not want to move.

The arbitrator upheld the company's right to move (and denied the union's right to walk out at Philadelphia), but he contended that it was wrong for management to make so momentous a decision without discussing with the union those matters which affect so directly the job security of its members. He went on to say that "a company in difficulties should in common sense terms discuss those matters with the union—it had a moral duty to discuss the matter" because, among other reasons, the workers might have ideas and suggestions that might "cause the company to alter or reshape [its] plans—or at least alleviate the harsh impact of the removal."

The arbitrator was not satisfied with the amount of severance pay offered to those workers who did not move. He increased the sum, taking into consideration their length of service, age, and opportunity for other employment. "The impact of a removal of a plant upon the lives of the employees and their dependents is sharp and severe both financially and emotionally. . . . In concluding to make the removal, the employer must count as part of the cost . . . adequate provisions to the employees where jobs are involved."

In sum, the arbitrator did not question that the company had the right to move part of its business from one plant to another in the expectation of adding to its efficiency, but, he said, the company faced two obligations. It must consult with the union because of the drastic effect of such a move on the lives of the workers; and it had an obligation to be generous to older workers who might be permanently unemployed as a result of the move. These were costs incident to the move that the company had to cover.

Quite different was the case reported in the New York City

newspapers in July, 1960, of a textile manufacturer who, despite being party to an agreement between an employers' association and the union prohibiting any member from relocating without engaging in collective bargaining, disappeared from sight during the course of a weekend. After his workers had finished their week's work on Friday afternoon, he packed and shipped all of his equipment to Mississippi. When the workers reported for work on Monday morning, there were no jobs, no machines— in fact, no company. The arbitrator awarded the union $200,000 plus additional funds to cover pay losses while the equipment was being returned from Mississippi to New York. His award was appealed to the courts where it was upheld. The judge was indignant about the "use of stealth." He held that management had not only broken its contract but had also acted immorally.

The U.S. Court of Appeals, Second Circuit (New York), decided two important cases in the spring and summer of 1961. One involved the relocation of a bindery from one community to another in upstate New York (*NLRB v. Rapid Bindery*); the other involved the relocation of a food processing plant from Elmhurst, Long Island, to Bethlehem, Pennsylvania (*Zdanok v. Glidden Co.*).

In the bindery case, the Court agreed with the basic order of the National Labor Relations Board (NLRB) that all employees who had lost their jobs by virtue of the closure of the plant and the removal of the work to another location be offered "immediate and full reinstatement to their former or substantially equivalent position without prejudice to their seniority or other rights and privileges." The Court emphasized that "Since the move was made through a legitimate exercise of managerial discretion the employer was not obligated under the National Labor Relations Act to have submitted it for discussion at the collective bargaining table." The Court emphasized that, when a change or discontinuance of business operations "is dictated by sound financial or economic reasons," there is no violation of the Act even if the employer's decision to relocate has been influenced by his desire to escape from a union. But the Court found, however, that the company was in violation of the Act because of "its failure to give notice to the union of the move and failure to discuss the treatment to be accorded displaced employees." It drew a sharp distinction between "the decision to move [which it held] was clearly within the realm of managerial decision" and the necessity to inform the union once the decision had been reached. In the Court's words, "Nothing affects conditions of employment more than a curtailing of work, and such a curtailment is properly the subject of collective bargaining."

The Court went out of its way to affirm, not once but repeatedly, that it recognized management's right to decide unilaterally where it could produce most efficiently. But it insisted that the exercise of this right did not permit it to escape its obligations toward its employees with whom it had signed a collective bargaining agreement.

The same Court, but in a divided opinion, went considerably further in making explicit the rights of long-term employees in the face of the removal of work from Elmhurst, Long Island to Bethlehem, Pennsylvania. Although the agreement between the union and the employees had expired, five workers, between the ages of 43 and 61, with between 10 and 25 years employment, sued to have their seniority and rehire rights protected at the new location. The company had offered to give fair consideration to applications for employment at Bethlehem of former employees at Elmhurst on the same basis as new applicants. But seniority would not carry over.

The company contended that the employees had "no rights which survived the contract," but the Court refused to sustain this position, especially in light of the fact that the company was paying retirement benefits under a non-contributory plan. In the Court's view, retirement pay was a vested right and, by the same token, these employees had "earned their valuable employment insurance and . . . their rights in it were 'vested' and could not be unilaterally annulled."

The majority opinion went on to say that "We can see no expense or embarrassment . . . from the [company's] adopting the more rational, not to say humane, construction of the contract" which, in the judges' opinion, remained in force even after the company relocated its operations. The Court found that the employees "were entitled to be employed at the . . . Bethlehem plant with the seniority and employments rights which they had acquired at the Elmhurst plant." Chief Judge Lumbard, in his dissent, agreed with his colleagues that "relocation of an employer's plant does not of course automatically terminate all rights under collective bargaining agreement" but he contended that the issue here was "whether this . . . agreement gave the employees the right to 'follow the work' to the new site" and held that it did not.

Once again, the Court did not want to interfere with management's prerogative to decide where it could best carry on its operations but the majority felt strongly that the right to relocate could not abrogate employees' rights acquired through years of service. If management wanted a free hand at Bethlehem, it would have to bargain with the union with respect to these vested rights. Employers have already begun to seek to protect themselves from this continuing obligation by writing into their agreements an explicit provision that in the event of relocation seniority will not govern.

Shortly after this opinion was handed down, the U.S. District Court in the Eastern District of Michigan pushed the emerging logic a step further in *Oddie v. Ross Gear and Tool Co.* The facts are simple. The company decided to close its Detroit plant and move all the work to Lebanon, Tennessee, where it had entered into a long-term lease for a facility which had been built for it after a promise that it would hire only local labor. The judge formulated the issue thus: "Do seniority rights survive . . . as an earned right?" He concluded:

1. That the collective bargaining agreement grants the employees certain benefits and rights that become "vested" in the sense that they cannot be unilaterally denied.
2. That these rights extend beyond the time limitations of . . . agreement.
3. That these rights apply to a "plant" regardless of . . . location.
4. That these rights include, among other things, seniority rights in rehiring and layoff (which go beyond an anniversary date) as provided in the contract.

The judge concluded, therefore, that the company has an obligation and duty to rehire on the basis of seniority those employees laid off in the Detroit area when that plant's operations are removed to Lebanon. The Circuit Court reversed but on the narrow ground of the coverage of the contract.

In October, 1962, the Supreme Court refused to review the substance of the Elmhurst case, thereby underscoring that in the exercise of their managerial prerogative to relocate, employers must meet their commitments to workers who have earned various benefits and rights. Moreover, to the extent practical, employers will be under mounting pressure to cover at least some of the more severe costs visited on older workers who will not be able to relocate.

Specialization

The issue of subcontracting, as it has been dealt with by arbitrators and judges in the last years, provides important insights into the exercise of managerial initiative when it comes to buying or making items or services essential to the enterprise. Before examining selective case material, it is necessary to set out, at least briefly, some of the major conflicts in philosophy that have been revealed in connection with this particular issue.

Until recently, it was held that, in the absence of a specific clause in the collective bargaining agreement with respect to subcontracting, the issue was not subject to arbitration, for decisions in this area fell unequivocally within the reserved powers of management to manage. Writing in 1959, an experienced arbitrator, Allan Dash, after making an exhaustive study of the subject, remarked that he was "fully persuaded on the basis of [his] study, that the large majority of the courts that have ruled on the arbitratability of sub-contracting work under agreements containing no provisions relating thereto, have ruled and will rule such issues to be non-arbitrable."

But the Supreme Court soon thereafter proved his prophecy wrong. In deciding the case of *Steelworkers v. Warrior Navigation Co.*, the Supreme Court found that although the contract between the Steelworkers and the Company contained a clause that "Issues . . . which are strictly a function of management shall not be subject to arbitration"; although the union had sought but failed in repeated efforts to include a clause limiting the company's right to subcontract in the agreement; although both the District Court and the Court of Appeals (the latter by a divided vote) had ruled that the issue was not arbitrable— despite these facts, the Supreme Court found by a vote of 7 to 1 that the matter *was* arbitrable. Justice Black took no part in the consideration or decision and Justice Whittaker dissented. Speaking for the Court, Justice Douglas made the following major points: a collective bargaining agreement is an effort to erect a system of industrial self-government; an order to arbitrate a particular grievance should not be denied unless it can be said with positive assurance that the arbitration clause is not susceptible to an interpretation that covers the asserted dispute —doubts should be resolved in favor of coverage; collective bargaining agreements regulate or restrict the exercise of management functions—they do not oust management from the performance of them; when an absolute no-strike clause is included in the agreement then everything that management does is subject to the agreement; "strictly a function of management" must be interpreted as referring only to that over which the contract gives management control and unfettered discretion.

With regard to the last statement, Justice Whittaker remarked, "This is an entirely new and strange doctrine to me. . . . it defeats both the contract of the parties and the controlling decisions of this Court." Here, perhaps, is a clue to why Mr. Dash's prophecy was proven false. His own analysis had cast a shadow ahead of the Court's decision: "In not a single published arbitration decision that I have discovered has an arbitrator ruled a subcontracting issue to be nonarbitrable." Once the Court adopted a strongly positive view toward the central role of arbitration in the maintenance of industrial peace, it was likely to defer increasingly to the judgment of the arbitrator which, in point of fact, was the concluding statement of Justice Douglas's opinion: "Whether contracting out in the present case violated the agreement is the question. It is a question for the arbiter, not for the courts."

The issue on subcontracting is joined because a union in entering upon a collective bargaining agreement with an employer accepts certain conditions of work for its members and the employer remains faced with the challenge to get his work done in the least costly manner. In pursuing this objective, he may, if he resorts to subcontracting, run afoul of the substance of his agreement. For in subcontracting, the work and wages about which he bargained may disappear—in fact, the bargaining unit may be seriously weakened or destroyed because its members no longer have the opportunity to work. And so, in this as in many other areas, workers' rights under collective bargaining and the right of management to manage come into conflict.

The simplest case for the arbitrator is one where the company clearly acts in a manner to destroy the unit with which it has a contract. Some years ago, the Celanese Corporation decided to subcontract its cafeteria operations. The subcontracting unit turned around and offered the Celanese employees their old jobs at markedly reduced wages. The arbitrator in this case was Allan Dash. He remarked in his opinion that "it is implied in every contract that there will be good faith and fair dealing and that neither party will do anything that has the effect of destroying or injuring the right of the other party to receive the fruits of the contract." The arbitrator pointed out that the company was operating in a distress area and that if it could subcontract it might make substantial savings in many other branches of its business, such as the spinning and other manufacturing departments. The company sought to parry this point by stressing that it was in the textile and not in the food business and that it was subcontracting work that was only peripherally related to its business. But, to this, the arbitrator replied that "the maintenance of plant feeding facilities is necessary to a successful operation by the company." Had it not been for the depressed economic conditions in the area and the jeopardy that subcontracting placed on the bargained for wages, the decision might have been in favor of management on the ground that the company was not in the restaurant business.

A much narrower issue was arbitrated in the case of the

Kaplan Furniture Company of Cambridge, Massachusetts. The contract provided that no work would be sent out unless all workers were "fully employed." At the time the contract was signed, the workers were employed 44 hours a week. At that point, chairs were being made elsewhere. Later on, the company sent out tables, but employees were then working 40 hours. The workers contended that "fully employed" meant 44 hours, not 40 hours. In the absence of any reference to 44 hours during the negotiations, the arbitrator held that the regular work week was 40 hours and that management was free to subcontract any work once it provided its employees with the guaranteed mimimum in the contract. The company's action did not jeopardize or destroy any basic aspect of the agreement.

A more complicated situation was presented by a conflict in the Krey Packing Company. The company moved into new quarters at which time it had an opportunity to subcontract for janitorial services provided by the rentor to all tenants at an estimated annual savings of about $7,700 which was the equivalent of the profits on an additional $1.5 million of sales.

The company pointed out that it was in a tight profit squeeze and that it had to take every possible step to reduce costs in order to survive. While the arbitrator was sympathetic to the company's efforts to cut costs his decision went against it. He pointed out that had the company rented new quarters and had the rent included janitorial services there would have been "obvious need" to eliminate the janitorial personnel. But in the present instance there was no overwhelming business reason for management to be permitted to eliminate the jobs of an entire work group through subcontracting. Management would have been granted relief from the terms of its agreement if janitorial services had been included in its new rent. But such was not the instant case. It could not use relocation as an excuse to deny work to a group who were covered in its agreement.

But when the Reynolds Metal Company, in 1959, converted a building from manufacturing to storage, removed the equipment, and shrunk the work force to a bare 12 persons, the arbitrator did permit it to subcontract guard functions through the installation of an electrical protection system. He pointed out in his decision that a collective bargaining agreement "contains no guarantee on the part of the employer to furnish employment to any individual or to continue operations." But he was quick to add that it did require him in the advent of reducing or eliminating work to show "good faith and reasonableness" —which in this case would mean letting out work for sound economic or business reasons. Convinced that the decision to subcontract was made exclusively in response to a major change in the business carried on at the location and "for no other reason" the arbitrator upheld the company's decision.

In the spring of 1959, arbitrator Harry Platt decided several cases between Republic Steel and the Steelworkers, all of which dealt in one fashion or another with the right of the company to subcontract where such action would leave the company's own employees unemployed or on a reduced work week. It is well to note as background that because of rapid technological and market changes, the employment trend in steel has been declining for some time, and the decline had been accelerated by a reduction in over-all economic activity.

In the first case, the arbitrator found that since the company did not possess the heavy equipment required to do a specific repair job and that it had little opportunity to hire it; and since its own employees could probably not have handled such equipment efficiently, it was reasonable for the company to contract out such work.

A second case arose because the company had introduced

improvements in its open hearth operations. Previously, the work had been divided between its own employees and those of a contractor, but the new process no longer required the initial screening and separation of the slag. The slag could now be pushed directly onto the pit floor where it was sent to the contractor for processing. "This substantial decrease in work had nothing to do with the contractor. It was primarily the result of a management decision to cease using thimbles." There was no question of management's right to introduce the technological change. The fact that its employees had less work than previously was no violation of the contract.

In the next case, the company subcontracted to remove and replace a fire-gutted roof. At one stage of the operation, the company's carpenters were working only four days a week; the contractor's, five days. This was the grievance. The arbitrator denied it on two counts: the contract had been let several months before the company's carpenters had been reduced to four days' work. But, more importantly, he questioned whether they would have been able to do the work since the contractor's men had sheet metal skills and after removing the wood immediately replaced it with iron sheeting. "In these circumstances I doubt that it would have been practical to separate the two phases of the job. Yet the union claims only the removal of the old roof for its carpenters." The arbitrator would not unsettle a preferred method of getting the job done simply to provide the company's carpenters with a full week's work.

In two other cases, also decided in favor of the company, the arbitrator stressed the integrated nature of many production and construction processes and the impossibility, without raising costs excessively, of dividing the work among two different groups of workers with different supervision. The other point which he stressed was the inability of business to enter into long-

term associations with contractors and then, because of a reduction of work for its regular employees, to go back on such
long standing arrangements. Agreements with contractors entered into in good faith cannot be challenged by a union when
its members happen to be on short time. A businessman has
the right to divide his work logically between his own employees and a contractor and he is under no compulsion to alter
his long-standing contractual relations whenever his own employees are on short time. At first glance, it might appear that
there is little protection to a union in signing an agreement with
an employer if he has the right to alter the way in which he
performs his work so as to reduce or eliminate the work of its
members during the course of the agreement. But such an interpretation would be false. It all depends on what the employer
does and how he goes about doing it.

In none of these cases was the security of the bargaining unit
an issue. The nub of the question in these cases was how far
should management be forced to deviate from a rational way of
organizing its technical processes in order to protect the jobs
of, or provide a full week's work for, its regular employees. The
answer was clear: not very far. The logic of production emerged
the victor over maximum job security.

We saw earlier, and we will see again in the case now to be
considered of the *Stockholders Publishing Company v. Newspaper Guild*, that clear economic advantage to the employer
even if he is in difficult financial straits may not be sufficient
justification to subcontract. The company sought to subcontract
for janitorial services and discharge nine janitors which, it estimated, would save about $10,000. The company argued that its
collective bargaining contract did not "exclude economies of
a just and sufficient cause" and added that it had better stay in
the black "and thus preserve the institution which gives support

to many persons and their families." The fact that the company had been in the red for three years and had had to discontinue an early morning edition indicated its precarious position.

Despite its vulnerable financial position, the arbitrator held against the company. "The Arbitrator wishes to emphasize that this decision does not deprive the Publisher of any chance of relief in its present financial plight. The decision merely holds that the Guild is entitled to a voice in the determination of what steps should be taken, to the extent that they involve employees which it represents."

This is an echo heard through many cases. The arbitrator finds against the company not on substantive grounds but solely because it has failed to consult or bargain with the union with which it has a contract. No arbitrator is insensitive to the imperatives of production or the balance sheet, but they are sensitive, just as the Supreme Court has indicated it is, to the simple fact that basic to collective bargaining is joint consultation. If work is going to be reduced or eliminated by relocation or subcontracting or through other means, surely the union which was established and is maintained to protect the jobs of its members should be consulted. To the extent that consultation represents a diminution of management's rights—and only to that extent —do these cases indicate any infringement on management's right to manage.

5. Management's Search for Efficiency

In an economy characterized by rapid technological change, a management must develop the skill and flexibility necessary to keep it in the vanguard or it will sooner or later be unable to compete successfully. One of the major challenges to management has long been—and continues to be—to organize its operations in such a manner that its use of resources is as efficient as possible.

When the management of a manufacturing enterprise installs a new machine that will result in a reduction in the number of workers required to perform a particular operation, the magnitude of the change is clear for all to perceive. There has never been any serious question of the right of management to purchase and install new equipment. The shady areas relate to the employment rights, under the terms of a collective bargaining agreement, of the affected work group—and others who in turn may be affected by personnel reassignments.

The installation of new machinery is the extreme case. Management constantly confronts the possibility of introducing changes into the on-going work process with an aim of increasing efficiency. In almost every instance, such efforts involve it in altering conventional work loads, work rules, rates of pay, work assignments—actions which, to some degree, may have an adverse consequence on some workers.

It is management, as Justice Douglas pointed out in the Warrior case, that "hires and fires, pays and promotes, super-

vises and plans." But the Justice went on to point out that it
may exercise those functions freely only "absent a collective
bargaining agreement." And therein lies the rub. For management's search for greater efficiency frequently runs headlong
into the worker's concern with protecting his job, his pay, and
his privileges—all of which have been reinforced by virtue of
the collective bargaining agreement.

Of course, all restrictions on management's freedom to change
unilaterally the process whereby work is carried out do not
date from the emergence of unions and formal labor agreements. In any work setting distinctions emerge about the types
of work to be carried on by different groups of workers, the
considerations to which different groups are entitled, the relative wages which they are to be paid, the quantity and quality
of work which they are expected to turn out, and all the other
factors that influence the efficiency of the work process. Such
conventional arrangements long preceded the rise of unions.
They are characteristic of every work situation. But, in recent
decades, because of the growth of collective bargaining, management has found itself confronted not only with tradition and
convention to which workers have always clung but also with
contractual barriers, the impact of which is being revealed only
slowly through the interpretations of the arbitrators and the
courts.

The analysis which follows sets forth the range of attitudes
and values held not only by the major participants as issues
about changing the production process are joined but also and
particularly those of the arbitrator, who in deciding the issue
before him, can never ignore the reality of a competitive economy in which gains in equity for the worker can never be secure
unless they are grounded in the efficiency and productivity of
the enterprise for which he works.

Several years ago, the management of the Pennsylvania Transformer Company sought to improve their operations by altering the standards of work required of employees engaged in arc welding. As a prelude to this change, the company undertook a time study analysis and set a new quota based on the results of this inquiry. The revised standard resulted in a required increase of about 20 percent in output without reasonable adjustment of the piece rates. The union submitted a grievance and won. The arbitrator was impressed that a substantial gain in output had been achieved without any "significant changes in the job," which was presumptive evidence that the contractual arrangements were being unsettled by the unilateral actions of management. Looking closer, he found that the time study had been deficient in several regards: only the steps in the welding cycle had been timed with no allowance for intermittent incidents; no "allowances" had been included, for instance, for delays in receiving the material; and the time of the best welder had been given disproportionate weight in setting the new quota. The arbitrator concluded that the new rates were not reasonable and that, if management was desirous of setting new standards, it would have to undertake a further study that would hold up under critical scrutiny.

A more complicated situation arose when the Murray Worsted Company introduced new twisting machines to operate alongside of old machinery. The company offered senior workers an opportunity to learn to operate the new machines but many refused because their earning ceiling would be sharply reduced—from a maximum of about $70 weekly to $46. Moreover, they would have had to change shifts. Several months later, the company laid off several senior machine workers while girls with much less seniority but who had been trained on the new machines continued to be employed. The company feared that it would suffer a serious loss in efficiency if it shifted workers with greater seniority but who were untrained on the new machines to work them. The company took the position that operating the two different machines represented different categories of work.

The arbitrator held that "the Company made a great error in not formalizing the separation (of jobs) in view of the basic rights (seniority) which might be jeopardized." In ruling against the company by insisting that it follow seniority in layoffs, the arbitrator added an interesting obiter dictum. Recognizing that the Company now faced lowered production because of the lack of training of the workers with seniority, he asked them to apply themselves assiduously to the performance of their tasks so as not to decrease further the profits of the company.

The situation was more clear cut in the case of General Baking Company when it introduced a new moulding machine which eliminated the need for a panner. The company reassigned the panner to new duties but the union objected. It argued that the panner could still be used to watch the gauges on the new machine and that such work was the heart of the efficient operation of the new machine. The arbitrator took a strong position in favor of the company. "The problems in the operation of the new machine are, however, even if real, the concern of the Company rather than the Union . . . in the absence of any restriction in its collective bargaining agreement." When there is a real change in the work process brought about by the installation of a new machine, he concluded, the organization of the work could be changed by management without prior negotiation with the union.

An issue which arose at Youngstown Steel was a more subtle one, affecting as it did a work practice that was on the way to becoming fully legitimized. It had long been customary on very hot days for the mill crews to discuss with their foreman a reduction in the rate of production required for the balance of the shift. In the present instance, the steward approached the foreman to request a slowing down of billets to be processed and received the reply that "he was to run the mill as he sees fit." He consequently reduced the flow of billets, but shortly thereafter the foreman decided that he did not want to run the mill at such a slow pace and sent the crew home. The union submitted a grievance and won. The arbitrator noted that, while management had the right to set the speed after taking the men's recommendations into account, it had failed to exercise its rights in the present instance and gave only ambiguous approval to a reduction. A worker could not be deprived of his pay because management was inept in exercising its prerogatives. Even under the most restrictive of collective bargaining agreements, management continues to enjoy a great many rights. However, if it fails to exercise them in accordance with the terms of the agreement, it jeopardizes them.

When the management of Seldner and Enquest, a chemical company, sought to exercise initiative in altering the plan of work, it found itself hobbled. The contract provided that, in the event that workers were employed for three days in one week, they were to receive pay for any holiday that occurred within that week. The workers worked Monday; Tuesday was Election Day; they worked Wednesday; and Friday was Armistice Day. The company stood to save two payroll days if it could complete its shipments on Wednesday. To this end, they hired extra trucks and were able to compress two days' work (Wednesday and Thursday) into one.

The company argued that Thursday's layoff was "dictated by economic considerations primarily and was therefore privileged and not in violation of contract." But the arbitrator held otherwise. "Holiday pay is an integral part of an employer's labor cost and wage structure. . . . Holiday pay is a prerequisite of the job subject only to contractually enjoined qualifications." He went on to add that proper and just methods to achieve economies of operation were not interdicted by his opinion but that the deliberate evasion of holiday pay was neither proper nor just.

Arbitrators are very sensitive to what might be called, in colloquial language, the "chiseling" proclivities of some managements who attempt to reduce workers' pay by exploiting special situations. At the Chrysler Plant at Dayton, a power breakdown occurred and the workers were sent home. The company knew, however, that later a truck would arrive that would have to be unloaded. When it arrived, it was unloaded by three employees from the service department, since the shippers had been sent home. The arbitrator upheld the grievance of the shippers: unloading was work which should have been available to employees in the shipping department; the shippers should have been permitted to do this work rather than have been sent home. The fact that the company knew that the truck would arrive was damaging to its case.

Much the same situation occurred at the John H. Mathis Company where a crane operator was sent home on a rainy day at 3:30 PM. At the time he was sent home, the company knew that a steel tank would arrive later in the afternoon. When it did, another worker was directed to operate the crane. The crane operator, who had been sent home early, submitted a grievance and won. The arbitrator held that management had "foreknowledge of need." In the case of a true emergency, management has the right to improvise, but even then arbitrators prefer to take a hard look to be sure that no worker is unjustifiably deprived of work to which he is entitled under the contract.

Such an emergency occurred at National Gypsum at its Niles, Ohio, plant on a snowy, cold Sunday at 12:45 AM. The power failed. The night watchman, remembering that he had the name of an electrician in his pocket as a result of a previous emergency, took it upon himself to call that electrician, who was the electrical group leader in the maintenance department. The senior electrician grieved and won. The company had instructed the watchman to call the senior electrician in the event of an emergency. The arbitrator commended the watchman for responding quickly and appreciated the fact that "he was not at the moment concerned with contract interpretation or the meticulous adherence to protocol, . . . the restoration of electrical power . . . was a critical necessity." Nevertheless, although the night watchman had acted promptly and intelligently, he had called the wrong man. The arbitrator held that the fact that the company had instructed him correctly was beside the point. He was the agent of the company and the company was liable for its obligations under the contract.

We have seen that arbitrators view with a jaundiced eye any and all efforts of management to take advantage of a situation to deprive workers of work, holiday pay, or overtime due them under the agreement. So, too, they will not support workers when their efforts have a clearly exploitative aspect.

At Youngstown Steel and Tube, employees on adjoining shifts had long enjoyed the privilege of relieving each other at other than formal shift changes. This was known as the "buddy system" and was one to which management had so long acquiesced that it was definitely a local working condition and, as such, was protected under the agreement. The passage of the Fair Labor Standards Act and the Walsh Healy Act, however, had introduced new criteria relating to the payment of overtime. As a consequence, the company found itself suddenly in a position where it had to pay frequently for overtime because of the "buddy system," because many were working more than the normal work week. Management sought to put an end to the arrangement and its action was approved by the arbitrator who held that it was federal legislation and not management that had, in fact, brought about the change. The old system "could be allowed by any employer without statutory penalties . . . but cannot without grave dangers of great penalties be permitted at this time." The arbitrator refused the union permission to use the new legislation as a vehicle to create overtime because of an accommodation that management had previously made without experiencing financial loss.

Similarly, the arbitrator upheld the action of the Shell Oil Company at its Houston, Texas, refinery when, during a fourth shutdown, it found it desirable to reassign operators to maintenance work even though it had not done so on three previous occasions. The arbitrator accepted the company's reasons for the change: many more workers were involved in the last shutdown. He held that "A custom with respect to a given situation is not binding with respect to other and different situations."

A last case involved an effort on the part of A. M. Beyers and Company to improve its maintenance program in 1957. This case underscored the sensitivity of the arbitrator for the rights of the workers under a collective bargaining agreement even when the actions of management are clearly predicated on an attempt to improve the efficiency of a work process. The established maintenance program was conducted by assigning workers to a particular area; the change involved a shift to a centralized system.

The arbitrator agreed that the old system was accompanied by inefficiencies that resulted in maintenance costs that were badly "out of line." The company argued that, under its contract, it retained the right to "direct the working forces," but the arbitrator held that the old system had the weight of a local working condition. "The Agreement's test for ruling on the propriety [of the change] is not whether the established way of doing things is inefficient or tolerable in terms of the Company's financial condition [but] whether the elimination of the 'local working condition' had been preceded by the removal of the basis for its existence."

The company claimed that, because it had brought up the subject of changing the system in discussions with the union, it had indicated its intention to abolish area assignments. This was not acceptable to the arbitrator who held that discussion was not the same as mutual agreement.

The company was not stopped from making the change, but the arbitrator held that it could not make it unilaterally. It would have to offer the union some concessions, for, by its actions, it would undoubtedly place some workers' jobs or earnings in jeopardy. A company cannot introduce changes in the work process solely because it can save money, even if savings are made more urgent by a poor financial situation, if such changes jeopardize workers' rights protected under the agreement.

A collective bargaining agreement permits management wide latitude in bringing about changes in the work process if the underlying technology is altered, but not if it suddenly or slowly becomes aware that it has been tolerating an inefficient way of getting work performed. In the latter instance such changes that it wants to make must be negotiated with the union for they involve threats to members of the work force whose security is protected under the agreement.

At no point does the arbitrator say that management is estopped from improving the operations of the enterprise within the framework of the negotiated agreement. He contended, however, that certain of its contemplated actions, particularly if they infringe directly on the jobs, or earnings, or other conditions of work protected by the agreement with the union, must be subject for discussion with the union and may be taken only if the workers' rights that are jeopardized become subject for a new bargain. In certain instances where management has a clear and unequivocal right under the contract to take certain actions, it will usually be upheld even if as a result of its actions the position of certain workers is worsened, even to the point of losing their jobs. But, in those instances where management's rights to act come into direct conflict with the rights of the workers to consideration under the contract, the arbitrator is forced to balance efficiency against equity.

6. An Effective Work Force

The self-employed person has responsibility for determining for himself how long and how hard he will work, how he will divide his time and energies as between increasing his current output and deepening his skills so as to be more productive in the future, and otherwise acts as his own supervisor. But in large organizations these and related responsibilities fall largely to management. In this chapter, we will review case materials that relate to assignment and training, supervision, and promotion and discipline—all of which reflect management's efforts to increase the effectiveness of its work force. But these efforts, as we shall see, are bound by the constraints exercised by the trade union's concern with equity for the worker. It is frequently the arbitrator's task to find a balance between the two.

These particular issues came very much to the fore early in this century at a time which saw the emergence of scientific management. A group of farsighted engineers perceived that large gains in efficiency could be achieved if steps were taken to make the work process more rational. They understood that by making it easier for workers to perform their tasks, by altering prevailing methods of supervision, and by the introduction of bonus systems, it might be possible to vastly increase workers' output.

Over the years, American management has become increasingly aware of the potentialities that exist on this front and it has devoted much time and effort to exploring the different ways in which it might call forth more effort from the members of its work force. At a minimum, it has sought to prevent their falling below standards which they previously had been able and willing to meet.

While early in this century management still failed in many instances to make significant distinctions between labor and other resources, the passage of the years has made it increasingly aware that labor is a unique resource. Since men have values and goals, workers cannot be manipulated, as can bricks and mortar, toward the sole end of utilizing them more efficiently.

Despite the considerable differences between labor and management in their respective attitudes, aspirations, and actions concerning work, the fact remains that when a worker accepts employment he obligates himself to devote his energies and his skills to the tasks to which he will be assigned. In return for wages, he promises to give a fair day's work—and fair means the generally accepted standard.

Management seeks to increase the effectiveness with which workers perform by trying to assign them in accordance with their skills and interests; by providing training when necessary to enable them to meet the specific demands of their jobs; and through exercise of supervision, appropriate discipline, and reliance on rewards. To the extent that management is skillful in the performance of its critical functions—assignment, training, supervision, discipline, and the use of rewards—it is likely to have an effective work force.

We shall soon see in this, as in the two preceding chapters, that the scope for managerial initiative while large is not unlimited. Even in the absence of a collective bargaining agreement, there are considerable limitations on management's scope for action, particularly in a large corporation. In large organizations, rules and procedures must play a significant role in the ordering of behavior. It is not possible for a large organization to rely on the personal decisions of a great number of different individuals, operating in a great many different spheres. While most large organizations make a strenuous effort to permit individuals at lower levels of supervision as much discretion as possible, the degree of discretion is limited because of the overriding necessity to insure a broad adherence to basic policy and to avoid decisions that might establish new precedents.

Whatever the margins of discretion might be in the absence of a collective bargaining agreement, it is inevitable that they will be considerably reduced by a strong union. For high on the priority list of workers' goals has long been a reduction in the arbitrary actions of employers who, in the absence of countervailing power, have frequently penalized or dismissed workers for trivial or even no cause. The commitment of labor to cut down this arbitrary power as rapidly as possible and to gain an even greater voice for itself in the determinations that are made in the arena of work is deeply rooted.

One of the more dramatic changes that have been under way for a long time in the American economy and that is still continuing is the shift from reliance on overwhelmingly unskilled workers to labor which has acquired varying degrees of specialized competence. Unions have sought to protect the job security of long-time employees by securing agreement in their contracts that, in the event of a decline in employment, workers with seniority are to be moved into jobs of workers with lesser service. And they have sought to give added value to this right by securing further agreement to the effect that management would provide some, or even considerable, training to enable senior workers to qualify in their new jobs. Management has, however, sought to restrict the scope of such "bumping" because it can lead to great unsettlement in work assignments. To protect one man's seniority has led on occasion to as many as 1,500 job changes.

One case that came to arbitration a few years ago involved a worker with seniority rights who was laid off after he had been given a two-hour trial on a new job. He had been given one hour's instruction and one hour's opportunity to show whether he could handle the new machine. The company considered that it had met its obligations under its contract. Not so the arbitrator: "I cannot frankly agree with the Company."

But a brief trial period may be sufficient if there is nothing to be gained and something may even be lost by prolonging it. An older worker, having recovered from a fall but unable to handle his old job, was shifted to several new jobs none of which he was able to handle satisfactorily. Finally, he was tried on a job where the contract stipulated that there would be a 40-hour trial period. Management, however, laid him off after a single shift because, in its opinion, there was no prospect of the worker being able to qualify even after 40 hours of training. Its action was upheld. The arbitrator said, in his decision, that "the idea of a trial period is a good one . . . it settles issues of qualification in a seniority bumping. However, the procedural requirement may be excused when circumstances make compliance dangerous or futile."

There are other times when procedural requirements appear important to the arbitrator and where compliance with them must be in spirit as well as in form. One company had followed all the required steps when it reassigned a sixty-year-old coiler first to a "lipe" coiler and then after eight days to a "number five" coiler because he had not been able to master the "lipe" coiler. The old man had difficulty in understanding English but he had received considerable help in doing the set-up work from an engineer, the set-up man, and a foreman. When the union complained about his reassignment to the "number five" coiler, the company put the man back on "lipe" coiler "in order to provide another opportunity to appraise his ability to operate (it)." There followed slow setups, errors, and a chipped cutting blade, although there was some question as to whether the broken cutter may have been caused by a broken cam shaft rather than by human error.

In his evaluation, the arbitrator found that management had met all the procedural requirements about assignment except the "spirit of the law." Engineers and foremen alike had brought a spirit only of levity to the matter. They had joked about "old Felix" whom they had decided was too old to teach. He had not really been given serious training because they had prejudged his ability to learn.

As this case suggests, management has the right to supervise; but, if it fails to exercise this right properly, it runs the risk of not being able to hold workers responsible. Workers are entitled to reasonable supervision; and, without it, they cannot be expected to meet reasonable performance standards.

In a pattern cutting corporation, management realized after several years that one of the women cutters was wasting between $35 to $100 daily through inefficiency resulting from incorrectly placing the patterns on the cloth that was to be cut. There was no argument about the facts. The woman cutter had cost the concern, which was in poor financial position, thousands of dollars over the past several years through spoilage. But the facts that were elicited at the hearing pointed up that she had worked under the nominal control of a mute foreman and that she had received very little supervision. The arbitrator saw fit to reinstate her for a sixty-day probationary period. The arbitrator, here, was apparently unwilling to put aside the long and sustained failure of management to provide adequate supervision.

What these few cases clearly demonstrate is the interdependence between the worker's effective use of a right given him under a contract, or implicit in an employment situation, and the behavior of management, as for instance in affording him an opportunity to acquire a particular skill. The obverse is also true: that management's rights to competent performance on the part of its work force can be placed in jeopardy if it fails to properly discharge its supervisory functions.

Arbitrators will usually go a long way to uphold the efforts of a responsible management to establish and maintain discipline in the work place. The California Electric Power Company discharged a competent operator, a Mrs. Miller, who had been given responsibility for instructing new employees because she broke a company rule that had recently been strengthened that no switchboard operator was to interfere with the lines of any other. When a learner, Mrs. Edwards, got on Mrs. Miller's busy circuit and started ringing in her customer's ears, Mrs. Miller shouted several times "get that out of there," and, when Mrs. Edwards failed to understand and comply, she leaned over and yanked her cords out. The hearing disclosed that the "Chief Operator," who together with her supervisor decided to dismiss Mrs. Miller, was engaged in tightening up discipline in the office and had aroused the hostility not only of Mrs. Miller but also of most other employees who had signed a petition for her removal. The arbitrator upheld the discharge saying that "the Company's decision to discharge Mrs. Miller was a bona fide exercise of judgment and discretion in an effort to maintain discipline and efficiency in the Inyorken office." Although the arbitrator recognized that there probably was bad feeling between Mrs. Miller and the "Chief Operator," "the fact remains that Mrs. Forrest was in charge of the office and had responsibility for maintaining discipline and efficiency and Mrs. Miller was subject to (her) jurisdiction."

In the case of a Minneapolis laundry where the management changed hands, friction developed between the washman foreman and the new owners. After some months, the new management warned the foreman in writing that if his work did not improve they would have to replace him. The company eventually took this action, largely on the ground that they had frequent complaints from customers that the clothes were not clean. At the hearing, the union was able to prove fairly conclusively that the number of such complaints was not excessive. And yet the arbitrator upheld the company. "I don't believe that the discharge in this case was justified by any single reason stated in the notice of discharge. Nevertheless I am satisfied that in the past months Mr. Colton manifested a general unwillingness to follow management's directions or to work with the new owners in correcting causes for complaint. . . . Because of their attitudes and consequent strained relations, . . . it would be difficult for management and Mr. Colton to get along together in any advantageous working relationship."

As noted earlier, the management will not be upheld if its own actions reveal that it has failed to exercise its guidance and supervisory functions properly. R. F. Paul, a jig builder at Convair at Fort Worth, Texas, was discharged shortly after he received his third of three "green slips," used by the company to warn employees of shortcomings in their work. Paul argued that the first two warnings had been "explained away" and that the third one followed his going out of channels to telegraph his Congressman that the "war-time supervision" in the tooling department was making it difficult for the older workers to hide their own deficiencies. The telegram elicited inquiries from

Washington and from company headquarters and the union argued that thereafter the company wanted to dismiss Paul.

The case of Paul's dismissal was "poor workmanship in the planning and fabrication" of a special tool that he had been ordered to design and build. The general practice is to give the jig builder a sketch that is prepared by a tool designer to guide him; a processor routes the parts to be machined; and the machined parts are delivered to the jig builder for assembly. "In this instance Paul was given no sketch, he had to design the tool himself and he also had to supervise the routing." In short, he received practically no assistance or supervision. The arbitrator commented that Paul had not received "assistance or supervision even approximating what was required under the circumstances . . . and that the seeming indifference (of the foreman) is almost incredible."

A much simpler case where managerial shortcomings helped to protect the worker from arbitrary dismissal occurred when a Mrs. Willman was discharged from the J. DeWitt Insulation Company of Kenova, West Virginia, after she had been given a chance to resign. She was discharged because it was found that she had been violating an explicit provision of the contract by spending time with visitors at her machine talking instead of working. However, she was reinstated by the arbitrator when he learned that a foreman from another department had made a practice of visiting her. While evidence was offered that these visits lasted for an hour or more, and although the company dismissed the foreman, the arbitrator held it important that Mrs. Willman had never been warned that her infractions of the rules might lead to dismissal. More importantly, these infractions were a direct consequence of lapses on the part of the foreman, and management was responsible for his behavior.

This brings us to the analysis of a series of cases that bear on the scope of managerial action with respect to promotion and discipline. The success or failure of management to develop and maintain an effective work force is much affected by the scope which it retains to promote the more able workers and to protect itself, in appropriate fashion, against incompetent or otherwise unsatisfactory employees. It has long been a complaint of management that a system of seniority is a major deterrent to efficient operations not because it gives enhanced job protection to older workers but because it prevents the selection of workers whom management would prefer to train and advance. Despite a seniority system, management still retains some measure of freedom in this circumscribed area—circumscribed by the union because for so long the exercise of favoritism by management had worked against the welfare of good union members. This is suggested by the case of the Dixie Cup Company.

The contract required that seniority govern in promotions where ability was equal. Management, nevertheless, appointed a junior man over a senior man who had bid for a job. The evidence adduced showed that the junior man had worked hard to qualify himself for promotion by learning many details about the new job. On the other hand, the senior worker had voluntarily shifted some time earlier from a more skilled and higher paying job to a less complicated one with less pay. Moreover, he had frequently refused to work on Sundays, preferring to spend the time with his family. The arbitrator's decision turned on the question of whether a worker's attitude toward work and promotion is a facet of the broad concept of ability and, deciding that it was, he sustained management. Contemporary research about motivation tends to support the arbitrator's accepting the assumption that differences in attitudes toward work will be reflected in differences in performance.

Important as are conflicts about promotion even more im-

portant are those involving inefficiency evidenced by workers
which can lead to penalties including their discharge. The conflicts usually include one or more of the following questions.
Did the worker actually perform ineffectively? Was management
responsible in some measure for his failure? Had the worker
any warning which would have alerted him to the necessity of
trying to do better? Was the penalty reasonable? There are two
further aspects which will be dealt with in later chapters that
bear on management's adherence to stipulated procedures for
disciplinary action. Contract enforcement, like law enforcement
in general, must follow established rules and procedures and cannot be arbitrary. But, in the assessment of responsibility, the
question of extenuating circumstances must also be considered,
for the worker is a human being first and an industrial resource
second.

The following cases bear specifically on poor work or improper conduct.

Except for a 15 month layoff after V-J Day, Kochensparger
had been employed by Curtiss Wright since 1942. His record
was free of complaints. He had been a final inspector for 20
months prior to the incident which led to his discharge in 1948.
The fin of an IXP87 aircraft had been damaged in transit and
in disassembling it for repair numerous unsatisfactory items
were found that had been made in "Department 3" where final
inspection and approval rested with Kochensparger. The Board
of Arbitrators found that the "approval of unsatisfactory workmanship could have resulted in the loss of pilot and aircraft."
In his defense, Kochensparger said that because of the quantity
of work which he had to review he was unable to give proper
attention to all of it. The Board gave no heed to this, stressing
again that in aircraft manufacture the lives of pilots and crews
are at stake. In fact, while the Board ordered the worker's re-

instatement because of his good prior record, it insisted that a penalty was proper "not only as a judgment against Kochensparger but as a warning to others."

The Board then considered whether management had placed the inspector in an unresolvable dilemma by asking him to check on an excessive amount of work leaving him, as his only recourse, to cut corners and to hope that he did not overlook anything important. The Board refused to countenance this excuse. Recognizing that faulty inspection could result in the loss of life, it acted to punish the man responsible, especially because he had not explored other ways of reducing the excessive demands on him. But it probably took this factor of an excessive work load into account in mitigating his punishment.

In sharp contrast, the General Controls Company in Los Angeles at about the same time suspended one of its thermostat inspectors, a Mrs. Holmes, on the ground that she was overscrupulous to the point of rejecting units that met acceptable standards. Her standards of workmanship were too high in management's view. Mrs. Holmes had a record of seven-years' employment, the last three of which were in the capacity of inspector. All of her ratings on employee review were very high.

After considering discharge but deciding that it was too severe a penalty, management suspended her for five working days for "gross carelessness," which was stipulated in the contract as a ground for discipline. The argument turned on whether the company had ever established the accepted tolerances for inspection clearly in writing; whether the test of Mrs. Holmes's work was scientifically valid; whether she should not first have received a warning; and, above all, what meaning should be attached to the term "gross carelessness." After a careful review of these several facets, the arbitrator decided that a written warning would have been the appropriate disciplinary action in the case of such a good worker, lifted the suspension, and made her pay whole.

But, when management can prove its case and its disciplinary action is temperate, it can expect to have its action upheld. The Dwight Manufacturing Company had laid off W. O. Boggs for three days because he had put the wrong loom beam on a slasher and had started to run it, which had resulted in a loss of about $50. Boggs testified that he had made a mistake and he was sorry for the damage and that he had never made this mistake before. The arbitrator held, however, that the layoff was reasonable. Boggs had received warnings for other mistakes and "it may be expedient to follow a warning with a stronger form of disciplinary action. While it is true that [his] action was not intentional there is no reason for overlooking his apparent laxness in attending to his duties."

A more intricate problem was presented in the discharge of Miss Couchenour by Curtiss Wright because of her inability to perform effectively as a paint inspector. She had worked as an inspector for five years but had been moved to the paint department only four days before her discharge. The transfer had been made because of a reduction in force. Miss Couchenour complained that the fumes made her nauseated and she indicated that she therefore did not want this job. While the Board of Arbitrators upheld the company's right to transfer workers within an occupational group, it stated that this "right carries with it the obligation of reasonableness. If the Company were without limitation, the Company could work the discharge of many employees by transferring them . . . and then discharge them because of the lack of qualification." The crucial conclusion of the Board was that "physical fitness is a factor in qualification." It was not unreasonable for Miss Couchenour to indicate that she did not like her new assignment since she was made ill by the odors. One cannot perform effectively if one is ill. In accordance with this line of reasoning, the Board ordered her reinstated in the job which she had held prior to being moved to the paint department.

When a man accepts a job, he takes upon himself a series of obligations about how he will behave during the hours when he is employed. At a minimum, he obligates himself to work during the time for which he is paid and to perform his work honestly. It is not surprising, therefore, that management's decision to discharge was upheld in the following two cases.

Paul Tiberi was discharged because he left his work four times during the course of one day to telephone and this consumed a total of 78 minutes. This amounted to approximately 20 percent of his entire working day. Although he pleaded that his wife was ill and that he had to make the calls in order to get somebody to help her, the arbitrator pointed out that he could have requested permission to make these several phone calls in order to make proper arrangements. The fact that he was an employee of seven-years' standing cut both ways. He knew the company rule about "killing time" and the penalties attached to violations. The union argued that the foreman had followed Tiberi to the phone the first time and had alerted the guard to keep track of him and that instead the foreman should have warned Tiberi. The arbitrator considered the question of entrapment and concluded that it was not involved.

The First National Stores were upheld in their discharge of a truck driver who had bought unnecessary amounts of gasoline on the road, had pocketed discounts, and had failed to check on the amounts which he did purchase. The union's rebuttal rested on the fact that his gas gauge was broken, but the arbitrator contended that this was less important than the fact that he had been driving the route for several months and therefore knew the capacity of his tank. The argument that discounts were a courtesy of the station to the driver and that they were the practice of the trade also held no weight with the arbitrator. He held that the pocketing of discounts would have been disapproved by the company and that the driver realized this but practiced deception. In this case, dishonest personal gain plus deception were strong enough grounds to justify discharge.

The complexity and the variability of human institutions and practices make it venturesome to draw conclusions about the scope of action within the province of management in establishing and maintaining an effective work force. But it may be useful to attempt a broad summary of the demarcations set by these decisions.

Management retains very wide scope in determining assignments and reassignments, training, promotion, and discipline of its work force. But its authority hinges in the first instance, under collective bargaining, on effective discharging of its responsibilities. Workers must be reasonably assigned; they must usually have a chance to learn the requirements of new jobs; they must be properly supervised; they must have a clear understanding of what they are required to do. If management meets these criteria, it will be upheld when it seeks to discipline workers for their shortcomings or failures. But management must always be careful to have "clean hands." Collective bargaining has sought to prevent the mistakes and errors of management from being visited on the heads of workers. The work contract is based upon a mutuality of responsibilities. To the extent that management meets its responsibilities properly, it remains in a strong position to insist that its employees meet theirs.

PART THREE
THE WORKER'S EQUITY

7. The Law of the Shop

In a modern democratic society, the amount of leverage which an individual or a group is able to exert on other individuals or groups with whom they may be in competition or conflict is seldom the reflection of a singular dimension. It is much more likely to encompass the totality of their rights and privileges that are derived from multiple sources. The American worker has certain rights by virtue of his history; others, as a consequence of his citizenship; and still others, because of his membership in a trade union.

The preceding chapters have reviewed various ways in which unions have been able to affect the rights of management by enhancing the rights of workers. However, only a part of the broadening and the deepening of the rights of workers in the recent past was the direct consequence of the growth of trade union organizations. Much is rooted in the changing patterns of political democracy and the extension of the rights of human beings through a deeper perception of the nature of humanity.

Noting these additional parameters, however, does not undervalue the contribution of the trade union in securing the gains that the worker has been able to achieve with respect to his job. One of the hallmarks of social progress is the establishment in law of rights not previously recognized or fully legitimized. That which comes to be deeply imbedded in the laws of people, especially a democratic people, assumes added weight and significance by virtue of becoming institutionalized.

Of even greater significance than the passage of a particular law is the development of a system of litigation and adjudication on which can be erected a system of self-government.

This is the true accomplishment of the union in the arena of labor-management relations. Over the past several decades, there has developed a system of formalized procedures for the control, reduction, and peaceful resolution of conflict. At the center stands the collective bargaining agreement with the union which includes a non-strike clause and a prescribed method for the handling of grievances which builds up through a series of stages to arbitration.

While the union has acted to protect the worker in a great many different ways, not only in the work arena directly but also out of it, no other accomplishment exceeds in importance what it has been able to achieve through the development of a formal system for the adjudication of grievances at the work place. The difference between the free man and the serf is the difference in the rights of each to plan and control his life. And since work fills so much of a man's life, his opportunity to enhance his freedom is through acquiring ever larger control over the conditions under which he works.

This chapter will seek to illuminate the significance of the grievance procedure as a formal system and to call attention to the important values that attach to procedural safeguards. Therein lies much of the value of collective bargaining for the worker. Therein also is the cause of much of the dissatisfaction of management, which believes that the procedures frequently are an unjustified impediment to the legitimate exercise of its authority to control the work force and insure efficient operations.

The importance of the collective bargaining agreement for the protection of the worker is illustrated by the case which involved I. Hausman and Son and Local 144 of the Display Union which came to arbitration by mutual agreement when Robert Bender was discharged from his two-day-a-week job of trimming windows for the Hausman shoe chain. The company stated that it was in such a poor financial position that it had stopped replacing employees who had retired or died and that it had even been forced to close out one of its choicest locations. The company had discharged Bender because he was a trimmer only. The arbitrator held that the company had the right to combine window trimming with selling. He went further. Since there was no contract, there was no seniority arrangement and hence Bender could not possibly be entitled to bump another worker. Similarly, there could be no layoff for Bender for that would clothe him with seniority rights. "Along the same lines I cannot award him severance pay," said the arbitrator. Without a contract, the worker was at the mercy of the employer—he had no seniority, he had no right to bump other workers, he could not be laid off with the prospect of preferential recall, he had no claim to severance pay.If the company made a decision to discharge him, it was acting within its rights.

In contrast, when Hersh's Department Store, a small retail establishment, sought to terminate the employment of one of its three salesmen because of a decline in sales, the arbitrator handed down a quite different decision. He accepted the company's claim that economic hardship necessitated a cut back in employment but he insisted that the seniority clause be respected. The company had wanted to retain a junior man whom it considered a better salesman. The arbitrator held that such action would be "to substitute the subjective standards of the employer for the single objective standard [seniority]. . . . It does not appear that the difference between the . . . two particular salesmen . . . is so great, or the disparity in their salaries is such as would cause the employer's insolvency were the principle of seniority not waived."

The arbitrator's language is revealing; not only does he consider seniority to be the only truly objective criterion but also he holds, in light of the agreement, nothing short of the threatened insolvency of the employer would lead him to consider waiving it. We see, then, that, under a bargaining agreement, a worker has substantial protection.

While the agreement, through seniority and other provisions, gives the worker valuable rights, it also places an obligation on him to follow stipulated procedures in order to realize his rights. Otherwise, management could be vulnerable to the troublemaker. If a worker fails in this regard, he may jeopardize his valuable rights. Here, indeed, is a close analogy to the law. The adherence to procedure is a necessary stage in the protection of substance. The way in which form and substance tend to be intertwined in the world of work and the importance of recognizing their interdependence is illustrated by a case involving the Ironrite Company. Foreman Benedict requested Gave, an oiler, to clean up a breech so that the tool makers could work on it. Gave stated that this work was not included in his job classification and discussed the issue with his steward who agreed with him. When informed of the steward's opinion, the foreman said that he would have to discuss the matter with personnel. The plant manager and personnel, pointing to the job description—"the oiler cleans machines and equipment"—disagreed with the steward who continued to hold to his position, buttressing it by stating that, in ten years, no oiler had washed down a machine.

On three successive days, the foreman ordered Gave to clean the machine. "If you don't I'll have to take further steps with you." Gave refused. He was given a disciplinary notice and on the following week was laid off for three days.

At the hearing, it developed that oilers had washed machines only during periods of experimentation and "as a favor." The arbitrator formulated the issue as: "whether an employee must accept an assignment from his foreman even though he sincerely believes that it is outside of his classification." His decision was that the employee must obey and then submit a grievance. The violation of the worker's obligation was a major one, he held, and called for a severe penalty. But since the parties had not previously had to cope with such a situation, since Gave was acting on the advice of his committee, and since his prior record had been good, the charge of insubordination would be removed but the penalty would stand. While management has no right to make "spot demands" on workers, in the event that the meaning of the contract is ambiguous, the safest position for the worker is to comply and then voice his grievance. Arbitrators are loath to uphold the right of a worker not to comply with management's orders. It may be that the law is on the worker's side, but he should not take it into his own hands.

Another interesting aspect of how procedure can contribute to the broadening and deepening of workers' rights is revealed by a series of cases based on the relation between infractions and punishments and on whether punishment should be based on the nature or the consequence of the infraction.

A case came to arbitration when an employee at Bethlehem Steel was demoted for unsatisfactory work one year after being assigned as a checker. He had committed a series of errors, which became more significant because there was no further inspection of the product. The company argued that its action was neither a demotion nor a disciplinary move but simply a reassignment of a worker to more suitable work in the interests of efficiency. The arbitrator refused to accept this interpretation, believing that the worker had the ability, but not the inclination to do his work properly. He held that the reassignment was in fact a demotion, with no termination, and that the employee should have been disciplined. If management fails to exercise its rights appropriately, it places them in jeopardy; it cannot wait a year to determine whether an employee is capable of performing effectively. A worker must also grieve within a stipulated period if he is not to jeopardize his rights under the agreement.

Another case was presented when Messrs. P. and B. were discharged from the Lockheed Plant at Burbank, California, for taking bets on company property and on company time. Most arbitrators, including the one in this case, hold that companies are entitled to protect themselves against practices that have an adverse effect on efficiency, such as those which waste time and, even more important, those which create bad feeling among employees. But the discharge of P. and B. was not upheld because, in the opinion of the arbitrator, the company had not acted "fairly or consistently." The fact that the company had waited six months in P.'s case and 18 months in B.'s case before discharging them appeared to the arbitrator to be "a tremendous time lag." He was also concerned about the discrimination which the company had exercised by acting against P. and B. who received the bets but not against those who had placed them. "The Company has established a double standard of culpability which is indefensible." Despite the arbitrator's opinion that the management had a right to act against gambling on its premises, he refused to uphold its actions in the present case because of its failure to follow reasonable procedures.

In law, the court usually determines the seriousness of the crime by the damage wrought, especially if a human being is injured or killed as a consequence of the act. A driver whose momentary inattention leads to the death of a pedestrian can be charged with homicide and can receive a long jail sentence. Under collective bargaining agreements, arbitrators are usually unwilling to explore the impact of the error or misdeed; they tend to limit themselves to the nature of the infraction and assess penalties accordingly.

At the Downington Iron Works, an employee was working on a new lathe. He failed to secure a piece in the lathe and when he began to turn it, the piece came loose, and did considerable damage to the lathe. His penalty was a layoff until the lathe was repaired. The arbitrator found that it was pure chance that the loose piece flew into the lathe; it could just as easily have been thrown clear in which case the worker would not have been subject to discipline. The idea that "the punishment should fit the crime" was rejected by the arbitrator. In his opinion, the error should be associated with the cause—the proper tightening of the piece, and not the effect—serious damage to the lathe. The arbitrator held that a civilized society should not mete out punishment on the basis of chance effects.

The management of the John Deere Waterloo Tractor Works in Iowa suspended Eddie Hanes for a week when he operated a gas truck without permission and while so doing seriously injured another worker. The arbitrator refused to uphold the suspension. It developed that Hanes, who was a good worker, had once received some training in driving a truck, and occasionally drove the truck although it was not clear whether the foreman knew this.

"In any event around 2 PM. on October 4, 1951 Hanes was moving Lawless' truck to get it under the flats so Lawless could load up. . . . Lawless somehow got behind the truck in such a manner that . . . the truck pinned or pinched Lawless against a pile of scrap, causing a severe injury to one leg and one forearm."

The union argued that Hanes was "disciplined without good and just cause . . . because other unauthorized persons have operated trucks without penalty in recent years." The arbitrator agreed with the company that "a rule is a rule" and should be obeyed. But he held that in the absence of the injury the only discipline, if any, would have been a warning. He held that Hanes should receive punishment appropriate to breaking the rule, not to causing injury.

Another aspect of the protection offered workers under a contract is that which stems from a requirement that management give proper notice about a reduction in work. At the Quincy Yard of Bethlehem Steel's Ship Building Division, the arbitrator found that the company owed back wages to a group of men who had been laid off without a forty-hour warning as provided in the contract. The issue arose because of a launching day. The company argued that the consequent reduction of work was not a layoff and that notice had been given since the men knew that a ship was to be launched. Cutting through a host of extraneous matters, the arbitrator held that "the employer knowing that the layoff was only for one day could have permitted employees to report and then send them home with only two hours' pay." A layoff is a layoff, whether it is for one day or many.

The Kroger Company which was entering the last stages of negotiations for a renewal of its contract with its truck drivers and fearing that it might not be able to reach a settlement before the deadline, canceled production to avoid a possible spoilage of $15,000 of baked goods. It gave its production workers as much notice as possible but less than the 12 hour warning provided in the contract. The union grieved that the work-

ers were entitled to pay because of a shift in starting time
without adequate notice. The arbitrator upheld the union: "The
company made a good faith effort to give the employees as much
notice as possible . . . and indeed . . . 57 of the 61 did not report for work. . . . The employees, however, lost a scheduled
opportunity for a day's pay, and also many will have been dis-
commoded." The arbitrator awarded one-half day's pay to the
aggrieved workers at an estimated cost to the company of about
$600. The company was able to protect an investment of $15,-
000 with an extra labor cost of $600; it should not have ex-
pected its employees to cover the risk.

But, where management is confronted by circumstances beyond its control and acts in good faith, it may be able to escape
the penalties of breaking a contract by failing to give adequate
notice. Legalisms are important but the arbitrator is even more
concerned about the underlying realities. The International Harvester Company closed its Melrose plant on short notice because
of a wildcat strike at its Tractor Works with which Melrose is
closely connected. The arbitrator upheld the company's right
to waive the three-day notice. "In view of the fact that the Company could have no possible motive for keeping secret a decision
to close, I cannot draw . . . the inference . . . the union
would wish."

The extent to which workers are protected by a strict interpretation of the conditions under which management is permitted to reschedule work is illustrated by a case that arose at
the Lukens Steel Company. In accordance with custom, the
schedule for the next week's assignments was posted on Thursday and it directed Peter Salitryonski to begin work on the
8 PM shift that evening. After the posting, the department supervisor noticed that Salitryonski had been on the 4 to 12 PM shift
during the preceding week. This would qualify him for over-

110 The Worker's Equity

time pay, since he would be working more than 8 hours within a 24 hour cycle. Accordingly, the supervisor changed his starting time to avoid this and Peter Salitryonski sued for 4 hours of overtime pay. The arbitrator upheld his claim. "Admittedly there is no requirement on the Company to provide overtime for its employees and good management requires that overtime should be avoided whenever possible to reduce operational cost." But the contract stipulated that indiscriminate changes "shall not be made in schedules except from time to time to suit varying conditions of the business." Management is not required to provide overtime but it cannot change schedules in the last minute to avoid it.

In exercising its right to discipline, management must have solid evidence of wrongdoing and must have warned the employee so that he will have had a chance of mending his behavior. Otherwise, its actions will not be upheld. This is demonstrated by the decision affecting a new employee at the Valley Dolomite Corporation. Donald House was hired on "a temporary basis" although the contract made no explicit provision for such a category. The superintendent asked House's foreman to observe his work and report any failure. He explained later at the hearing that he wanted to discharge the new worker if he failed to measure up during the ten-day probationary period. In point of fact, there was no such period; men acquired seniority from the day they were hired. On the ninth day of his employment, the superintendent asked the foreman how House was doing. The foreman reported that he had walked by House's work place eight times that day and on four occasions he had found him sitting down and not working. On the basis of this report, the superintendent sent for House and discharged him.

"On none of these occasions," said the arbitrator, "had the foreman or the Superintendent told House to get to work or asked him why he wasn't working. For all the foreman or the Superintendent knew, he was waiting for the arrival of tools or materials sent for. . . . It is quite evident that [the Superintendent] acted in this summary fashion because he was under the false impression that there was a probationary period during which employees could be fired with or without reason. Obviously the grievance must be sustained. The duties of the Company and the employees are reciprocal." The issue is not whether House was loafing or not; but simply that the company acted without adequate evidence and without having warned him to correct his behavior if it had been at fault.

Much the same opinion was reflected by the arbitrator who heard a case of three workers of the Copco Steel and Engineering Company who were suspended for three days for loafing on the evidence of a foreman who had walked in and out of the department about four times and had observed the men standing around and talking for at least ten minutes during each of these four visits. The superintendent had also noted that the men were standing idle for 15 minutes. In rebuttal, the leader of the three men testified that they had to wait to obtain a crane to lift and load the bundles on a truck. "It seems to me," said the arbitrator, "that if the circumstances were such as described, and considering that the men were not known to be habitual loafers, that it is supervisor's obligation to at least warn them of the consequences that would follow their failure to heed the warning." The company was entitled to a fair day's work but it was not entitled to be impulsive in its relations with its employees.

While many cases involving procedural matters are of relatively minor importance, others are crucial since they involve the worker's job. And if the labor market is slack, the loss of a job may amount to economic capital punishment, especially for an older worker. But the efforts of unions in this arena have had deeper meaning and impact. They have worked toward the establishment and strengthening of a system with procedural reenforcements, aimed at securing for workers the rights that they have secured under the agreement.

8. The Free Man

When a union signs a collective bargaining agreement with an employer, it commits the workers whom it represents to a voluntary restriction of their freedom—the time they spend at work —in return for which they receive wages and other important benefits. The restriction of freedom entered upon by the worker is of course limited as to time and place and is at no time complete. A mature democracy prohibits individuals from selling their freedom totally or permanently and prohibits men from depriving others of their freedom. Under our laws, a free man cannot turn himself into a slave; to that extent his freedom is circumscribed. Nor can a man buy another, even in a strange land, and bring him into this country to be held as a slave. All this ended a considerable time ago.

Under current law, an individual is permitted to place his time, energy, and intelligence at the disposal of another under conditions for which he has bargained freely. When an employment contract is signed, it carries with it restrictions on part of a man's day, not the whole of it; on some of his rights, not all of them. For those rights which he holds by virtue of his citizenship or by virtue of being a human being stand above and beyond the employment contract and they cannot be purchased or sold —at any price.

The thrust of this chapter is to investigate the conflicts that arise at the margin between the rights that are part of the patrimony of every citizen and those which he can suspend or transform for appropriate consideration arising out of his employment. The following chapter will parallel this treatment but will consider conflicts arising out of men's rights as members of humanity. The rights which a man enjoys as a citizen and as a human being are, of course, closely related and can frequently be distinguished only with difficulty.

In this chapter, we direct attention to three sets of cases. The first revolves around the scheduling of work which, as we will see, can have a compulsive influence not only on the pattern of life when a man is actually on the job but also on his life off the job. It is the latter segment of a man's existence that falls conventionally outside the control of the employer. The conflicts arise when the commitment made to the employer cannot be effectively fulfilled without disturbing a man's freedom to plan and live his life as he sees fit when he leaves the workplace.

Closely related to the problems of time are those related to the behavior of men off the job which cannot be completely disassociated from what they do at work. For man is one, even though his work and the rest of his life can be distinguished. A series of cases primarily involving the use of alcohol by a worker in his hours after work can help to illuminate the area of conflict between the rights of the employer and the freedom of the worker.

The third group of cases relates to the essence of citizenship because they involve the extent to which the individual's right to hold unpopular political opinions and to discuss them freely must be respected by the employer—especially if the voicing of such opinions introduces disturbance and turmoil in the work setting and lowers production and profits.

The way in which the exigencies of production can come into conflict with the desire of workers for order and regularity in their hours of work is well illustrated by the following case. The

Goodyear Tire Company was operating its Nailex and Accelerator work from Monday through Friday and was operating Nailex only on Saturdays. Consequently, the working hours of the department were changed from one week to the next. The men sometimes had three days off and sometimes only one. The workers objected to this week-to-week scheduling. Management's reply was that work flexibility was essential until the production program for these new products could be established. The arbitrator upheld management's right to change schedules because he found that it had, in fact, posted a monthly schedule from which it departed only for emergency repairs. The fact that management had posted a monthly schedule "proves that such scheduling does not impose any undue burden on the Company." The arbitrator held that the men were entitled to some schedule so that they "can properly plan their leisure time." Weekly changing of schedules makes it "almost impossible to make plans to participate in family affairs or to become engaged in any kind of outside social activities." However, he held that the monthly schedule adequately protects the men's freedom.

During the course of a year, many industries find that their operations must include peak periods of output which are followed by slack periods. This sometimes makes it advantageous for them to shut down completely for a period of several weeks, or even several months. Recent years have seen collective bargaining agreements provide paid vacations for workers of two, three, and even four weeks. Complaints have arisen about whether management can insist that the period of a shutdown be used as vacation time. This, of course, deprives workers of the choice of determining when to take their vacations. This was the problem presented by the action of the Phoenix Iron and Steel Company during the "rolling readjustment" of 1958. After having curtailed production in April, it shut down its

Phoenixville plant in May. Many who worked in April held lower paying jobs into which they had "bumped." When the Company sought to call the layoff period a vacation period, many of these workers lost money since the contract provided that vacation pay be computed on the basis of earnings in the first two of the last four weeks before the onset of the vacation. Still another group felt aggrieved because they were forced to be on vacation when they might otherwise have had a chance to work by bumping men on skeleton crews.

The arbitrator granted pay adjustments for all workers who had specified vacation dates prior to the shutdown. The arbitrator was not sympathetic to the company's claim that few would have been eligible for work during the five-month shutdown. He stressed that the workers "were not given an opportunity to express a choice" about when they preferred to take their vacation.

A related case arose at the works of Fairbanks Morse and Company when it sought escape from the difficulties presented by a staggered vacation program for a work force that was increasingly entitled to two or three weeks' vacation. In the fall of 1957, it notified the work force that the plant would shut down for two weeks the following summer. In the fall of 1958, it made the same announcement with respect to the summer of 1959, at which point the union grieved, contending that management's action was in violation of the contract which stipulated that "vacations shall be granted at such times during such periods as management and supervision shall find suitable considering both the wishes of the employees and the efficient operation of the plant, but every effort will be made to meet the wishes of the individual."

The arbitrator did not grant the company's contention that

it had a right to shut down. Moreover, he contended that, under the agreement, vacations should be "granted" not "ordered." "The vacation shut-down plan tends to ignore the wishes of any specific individual." While the arbitrator was willing to accept management's contention that "plant efficiency is improved by a vacation shutdown," he did not find the evidence conclusive that efficiency would be so impaired that a plan of staggered vacations should be disallowed. "Company convenience cannot be substituted for plant efficiency." "A vacation is used by different individuals for different purposes. Many such purposes cannot be served by a July vacation." Under the contract, the worker's preference must be considered; and it was this right that the arbitrator upheld.

In the past, workers at Kennecott Copper had been permitted to choose the time for their vacation, but a new agreement between the company and the Machinists' Union provided that "employees may be given their vacation during a shutdown." When management exercised this right, it was upheld by the arbitrator.

The Merck Company at its Elton, Virginia, plant was operating under a contract similar to that of Fairbanks Morse where the interests of both parties with respect to vacations had to be balanced: the company's need for efficiency and the workers' opportunity for choice. Management decided on a vacation shutdown, which was not contested by the union. A grievance arose out of the fact that management required workers in the maintenance department to work during the shutdown and to take their vacation during either the two weeks preceding or following the shutdown. Most of the workers in the plant, 110 out of 118, were entitled to three weeks which left all of them at least one week of vacation at their own choosing. Management was able to convince the arbitrator that there were sound operating reasons for requesting the maintenance men to work as scheduled.

The Chrysler Corporation, with much the same vacation clause, was not successful in convincing the arbitrator that sound operating reasons made it logical for workers to take one week of their vacation during a plant shutdown necessitated by a strike at Pittsburgh Glass. This strike, the company argued, would force a telescoping of operations when the plant resumed production because, among other reasons, the time of model changeover was approaching. Every worker would be needed. The arbitrator noted that "the wishes of the employees were given little if any weight. . . . There would have to be a compelling showing that the remaining non-critical weeks available to employees for vacation purposes were insufficient to accommodate . . . vacations." The arbitrator reviewed how the company had dealt with the requests of four employees for exceptions to the vacation policy: one was going to be married; another wanted his vacation later when his wife was going to have a baby; and two wanted to visit their parents. The fact that the company had given such short notice of its policy—twenty-four hours or less before the shutdown and that it had not responded sympathetically to all of these special cases probably weighed heavily with the arbitrator.

Sherwin Williams discovered that the 230 workers in its paint department were entitled to 688 man-weeks of vacation and that 472 were requested during the summer quarter of the year. This would amount to 45 men being on vacation each day during the summer months. If vacations were spread evenly throughout the year, it would amount to approximately 13 men on vacation each week. The company sought to permit the requested vacations as far as possible without seriously interfering with operations and posted a schedule which provided for 20 vacations per week during the summer period.

The contract contained the twofold criteria—employee's choice and orderly operations—for the scheduling of vacations. The union grieved that under the company's plan many workers were denied the opportunity of taking their vacations during the summer. It pointed out that through the liberal use of overtime, production could be made up. The arbitrator, reviewing this contention of the union pointed out that if the company took such action it would constitute a gamble. If a significant group of workers turned down the opportunity to work overtime, customers would be disappointed. He also noted that since senior workers received four weeks' vacation, additional difficulties would confront the company in attempting to have their skilled work satisfactorily performed through the overtime labor of less experienced men.

The fact that the company did not seek to remove all choice by closing down the plant, and the further fact that it had assigned a staff man for six weeks to work out a compromise vacation program was proof to the arbitrator that the company was neither arbitrary nor discriminatory. "The Company has sustained the burden of proof in this case."

The burden of these cases is clear. Whenever the contract provides for vacations that are to be scheduled with consideration for the worker's preference, management must make a serious effort to meet this criterion. It is not enough for management to prove that production difficulties will be created if the principle of choice is upheld. A vacation is a valuable right. But its value is enhanced if it can be taken when the worker prefers. It may not be practical to meet the requests of all workers, but management must attempt to meet the desires of as many as possible.

An allied scheduling problem that has led to conflicts relates to the work day, and particularly to the scheduling of overtime. While the issue appears to be of much less economic significance—involving hours rather than weeks—the conflicts are severe. Each of the contestants holds that the daily schedule comes close to first principles.

Some years ago, at about 3 PM one afternoon, the foreman at the Lockport, Illinois, yards of the Texas Company pointed out to Mike Dabrovich, who with Fred Taylor was loading roofing materials, the amount of work that still had to be done. Apparently, he did not give Dabrovich a clear order to stay on the job until it was finished and Dabrovich left the job at his usual quitting time of 4 PM. Dabrovich had not discussed overtime with the foreman since he noted that the foreman had just turned down Taylor who had made a request not to work overtime. The next day Dabrovich was suspended for refusing to work overtime. At the hearing, it developed that he was usually picked up by his wife at a street corner and that when the foreman discussed the work with him he was no longer able to reach her. The arbitrator acknowledged that the company had the right to require overtime but he held that in exercising this right it must give the worker reasonable notice. Dabrovich knew that his wife "would be waiting for him and the delay would cause her concern and anxiety. There is nothing unreasonable," said the arbitrator, "about his desire to fulfill the accepted routine." Moreover, "the Company found another to do the job . . . and the project was completed without undue delay and the car moved out. The Company was in no wise injured." Management's orders must be reasonable; this one was not.

A similar case occurred at the Ford Motor Company, when two employees were laid off for three days for refusing to work overtime. The penalty was reduced to one day for the worker who offered no reason for refusing; for the other who had an explanation, it was lifted entirely. The latter worker lived 15 miles distant from the plant and usually drove home with another worker. Had he had to use public transportation the amount of time required for him to get home would have been out of all proportion to the amount of overtime. While management has the right to require overtime, the arbitrator pointed out that "except when specifically so hired employees are not on continuous call 24 hours a day." Under their agreement, an employee may not refuse to work overtime simply because he does not want to work more than eight hours, does not need the money, or for no reason at all. But if the overtime work would unduly interfere with plans he had made, then his refusal may be justified. "A rule of thumb is not possible. What is required is sympathetic consideration of the individual's situation and make-up."

The decisions in the preceding cases indicate that despite its right to require overtime from its employees, a company must consider the impact of such a demand upon the ordering of their lives off the job. The next group of cases indicate that what employees do in their off hours may be a matter of concern to the employer about which he can take disciplinary action.

The Cleveland Pneumatic Tool Company was upheld in its right to suspend a milling machine operator for a week because during the first two hours of a shift he produced considerable less than the required standard resulting from the fact that he had come to work under the influence of alcohol. The union pointed out that this man was a valued employee who the night before had entertained his soldier nephews who were home on furlough. The union admitted that he had come to work fatigued but denied that his low productivity was a result of intoxication. It pointed instead to difficulties in the flow of materials.

The arbitrator accepted the company's version: the worker had had a thick tongue; he staggered and bumped his head; he had acted peculiarly; he had alcohol on his breath. "While it is true that what an employee does on his own time and while away from the plant is his own business, this general statement has certain recognized limitations. Where the employee's off-duty activities directly affect his work performance, then his conduct becomes a matter with which the employer may be properly concerned. . . . Where his work performance is thereby detrimentally affected to an appreciable degree, such conduct falls short of the obligations inherent in an employee relationship and in a proper case warrants disciplinary action."

A commercial representative of the Southern Bell Telephone Company was dismissed because of a series of incidents which indicated that he frequently had liquor on his breath. The arbitrator pointed out that "on a typical industrial job the Company will have no occasion for discharge . . . he is not alleged to have been drunk on the job; there is no claim that his work was adversely affected in a mechanical sense; and there were no customer complaints." But the discharge was upheld because M. "was in steady contact with the public and in regular business contact with other female employees of the company who might find the odor of alcohol offensive. The nature of the job is the critical issue in this case."

But this criterion can become obscured depending on the specific circumstances as the following two cases of Greyhound Bus drivers demonstrate. The company has a rule to the effect that any driver while on company property, or in uniform, or wearing part of the uniform, who shows any evidence of being under the influence of liquor is subject to discharge. The company wanted to protect its reputation as a dependable public carrier by this strict rule. Fred Borer, after operating a bus from Pittsburgh to Columbus, Ohio, picked up his pay check and went to the home of a fellow driver where he took some pills to relieve distress from a recent tooth extraction and had two or three shots of whiskey and two glasses of beer. Remembering that the next day was a holiday, he went back to the terminal to get his check cashed. While there, he became boisterous and argumentative. The safety inspector had the dispatcher suspend him and shortly thereafter he was discharged.

The Board of Arbitrators who heard the appeal upheld the company. It turned aside the union's claim that the company was trying "to regulate the private life of the drivers." Because the disturbance occurred at the Greyhound terminal, "the aggrieved driver laid himself open to the strong suspicion that he was a driver and that he was under the influence of alcohol." The board recognized, however, that "loss of livelihood is a serious penalty for one infraction of the rule" and it recommended reduction of the penalty. "This, however, is a matter of discretion." Since the public had no way of knowing that the driver who appeared drunk was not going to take a bus out, the Company had a right to protect its good name.

In the case of A. R., the discharge was not upheld although there was no question that he had had several drinks after a very long period of driving—18.5 hours out of a 21.75 hour period. A. R., after drinking, had gone to sleep in a company dormitory where, later, incontinence called attention to his condition. While the Board upheld the rule prohibiting drinking on company property, it pointed out that there must be some direct connection between an employee's act and a recognizable risk to the Company's business. The fact that A. R. had done his drinking at a veterans' hall and that he then went to sleep it off in the company dormitory kept him out of direct contact with the public. The arbitrators held that the rule must be applied with reasonableness. "It cannot be asserted to the degree of depriving a man of his livelihood if he partakes of a drink in the privacy of a place that is not open to the public, does not come into contact with the riding public in an intoxicated condition, and makes no attempt to go on duty while under the influence (not necessarily drunk) of intoxicants. The privacy of an individual driver's life cannot be invaded merely because of the existence of Rule G-32." The existence of a rule does not insure that it will be upheld. Its applicability to the case at hand must first be proved.

The Lamb Glass Company sought to dismiss a common laborer in its employ after he had been convicted in an Ohio court of drunken driving. The company contended that it had a rule against operating a motor vehicle while under the influence of liquor and further pointed out that the employee had failed to report for work on the day after his arrest and had failed to notify his foreman that he would not appear.

The union responded by denying that such a rule had ever been negotiated and asserted that it had never been disseminated. It claimed instead that it was unreasonable even to invoke such a rule in the present context since it was in no way related to the employee's work performance.

The arbitrator agreed with the union that "as a matter of 'common law' applicable to industrial relations, what an employee does on his own time is not subject to regulation by the employer" except under special conditions where good will is involved or where the employee cannot perform satisfactorily at his work. The failure of the employee to give notice of his absence is subject to discipline but the rule against drunken driving cannot be upheld. The worker was disciplined but he kept his job.

The most interesting set of cases about the rights of free men in the employment arena relate to what is broadly defined as "civil liberties." The following five cases take on heightened significance since they all date from the McCarthy period, when concern with the rising power of Communism caused many Americans to lose their perspective and to adopt the un-American doctrine that the end of security justified any and every type of defensive action including riding roughshod over the rights and liberties of free men.

The Firestone Tire and Rubber Company was upheld by a Board of Arbitrators in their dismissal of T. in 1951, on the ground that his incendiary attitudes and statements about American foreign policy caused considerable unrest which resulted in lowered morale and inefficiency. T. had had ten years' service with the company first as guard and later as a fire inspector. T. was an outspoken admirer of the U.S.S.R. and repeatedly announced his disapproval of United States involvement in Korea. The arbitrator asked, "does the law or the terms of the current contract obligate Firestone Tire and Rubber Company to retain an employee who insists upon repeatedly discussing subjects affecting national security with fellow employees that patently induce a condition of dissatisfaction, unrest, and anger among them . . . ?" The Board held that "an employee has no contractual right to harangue those who work with him on controversial subjects."

The Board thus contended that the Company had no obligation to furnish T. with a platform and captive fellow employees. In upholding the discharge, the Board felt that it did not thus interfere with T.'s right of free speech, but merely precluded him from talking within a certain locale and circumstances.

It must be observed, however, that the Board did uphold the discharge of an employee with ten years' service who had long voiced aberrant political opinions. The members of the Board were very responsive to the dominant values of the community which they largely shared. They made no effort to find a less extreme solution.

The Hayes Manufacturing Company of Grand Rapids, Michigan, was seriously embarrassed by one of its employee's political activities but in this instance, despite the fact that the Company was a defense contractor, the arbitrator did not agree to discharge as the appropriate penalty. Mr. G. asked for and received a 6 weeks' leave to go to Europe. It turned out that instead of going to Europe on a pleasure trip, G. joined 17 other professed trade-unionists to make a study of trade union activity in Europe, including countries behind the Iron Curtain. They visited Russia as guests of the government and participated in broadcasts and interviews. News of the group's activities was cabled home and G.'s role was played up in the local newspapers. The company canceled G.'s leave while he was still in Europe and shortly thereafter it discharged him, informing the union that "it would not reemploy G. under any circumstances." The company would never have granted him leave, it said, had it known the real purpose of his trip. The company informed the Navy, with whom it had contracts, of this action, which requested the company not to employ G. on any Navy work without specific authorization.

Harry H. Platt was the arbitrator and he took special pains in his opinion to sort out the multiple issues involved. He agreed with the company that G. had used deception to get a leave which, had the facts been known, would have been denied. Platt indicated that he was not conducting a hearing into "the political beliefs of the aggrieved nor a proceeding to punish him for holding unpopular views that may be abhorrent to his employer, the union, and to the arbitrator."

The company argued that its ability to secure defense contracts had been jeopardized by the publicity aroused by G.'s trip, which intimated that the company knowingly employed Communist sympathizers. Moreover, it pointed out, "Mr. G.'s activities have produced a considerable uproar in the plant." Finally, it contended that it had not discharged him but had simply canceled his leave and upon G.'s failing to appear for work, the company concluded that he had quit.

The union, in its reclaimer, stated that no proof had been offered that G. had violated any law; if he had, the union would want to reconsider its position. More importantly, it charged the company with trying to break down grievance procedures by using the current war hysteria. The contract provided that no discharge penalty could be meted out until it had been considered jointly by management and the plant committee, but the company had refused to discuss this case. On this issue of the company's violation of procedure, the arbitrator upheld the union. "It is the Arbitrator's firm conviction that in the long run the interests of both parties will be best served by requiring strict adherence by them to the terms of their agreement." Men should not lose their jobs because their discharge would be popular.

Mr. X., an employee of the Nine Mile Plant of the Chrysler Corporation, was discharged after he had been called before the Un-American Activities Committee and had repeatedly invoked the Fifth Amendment; there had been distributed at the plant under his name pamphlets of an incendiary nature; and there had been disturbances at the plant when he returned to work after appearing before the Committee. Many conflicting pieces of evidence were offered in testimony before the arbitrator who made no effort to sort them out. The Company was unable to establish that Mr. X had been directly involved in the distribution of the literature in the plant, and, without such evidence, the discharge could not be upheld since this was the declared reason for the disciplinary action. As in the previous case, the arbitrator refused to let passion take precedence over procedure.

But when management is subjected to serious risks because of the political attitudes or behavior of an employee, procedure may be minimized, and other values given precedence. P. and S., editorial writers for the Los Angeles *Daily News*, were named in sworn testimony before the Un-American Activities Committee as members of the Communist Party. The newspaper waited for the writers to clear themselves of the charge, and, when they failed to do so, it discharged them.

According to the arbitrator, the basic question is whether "the Publisher in self defense against anticipated serious financial repercussions brought on by unfavorable public opinion has the right under the terms of the working agreement to ask and expect those accused to clear themselves of the serious charges made under oath against them, if they are to continue their employment with the Publisher." He went on to state that "A newspaper is peculiarly susceptible to criticisms that flow from the supporting public. . . . It has a quasi-public responsibility to print the news without bias." The arbitrator saw no "censorship of the press . . . no infringement upon individual freedom. . . . Rather it is a simple forthright acknowledgement of our offices of public and semi-public trust in defense of our state and country against all the cunning and conspiracy practiced by present day communism."

When a journeyman linotype operator with a record of 13 years of satisfactory service on the *Long Island Star Journal* substituted the word "facism" for "freedom" in an address of the Secretary of the Navy, his discharge was upheld on the ground that it was not a normal error but rather one that suggested "willful substitution."

The abitrator was not impressed with the argument presented by the union that if the paper had had more proofreaders the error could have been caught. "I do not believe the paper should be under a duty to employ men just to catch the deliberate or mischievous mistakes of one of its other employees." While a democratic society must tolerate and protect political differences, no employee is entitled to jeopardize his employer's business by exploiting a position of trust and responsibility.

9. Human Dignity

In societies where most men are forced to struggle constantly for the bread they eat, there is little scope for anything else. Those values that are worthy of individual, corporate, and national concern and respect—those that reflect the potentialities inherent in men to give expression to such sentiments as charity, a sense of equity, and love for other men—can flourish only when at least a considerable minority is no longer locked in perpetual battle for daily survival.

The past decades have witnessed, both in the United States and in other advanced industrial countries, a deepening and a broadening of concern with aspects of men's lives, both individually and collectively that were previously given short shrift. The increases in total and per capita real income were a necessary, although not sufficient, condition for this development. The trend was manifested on many different fronts and with respect to many different aspects of the country's experience. Recourse was had to government to establish positive and negative conditions that would reduce, even if they could not eliminate a part of the individual and collective penalties that were previously attached to those who were less fortunate in the competitive struggle. Pressure was exerted on employers to humanize the work place so that some of the worst consequences of individual misfortune and ineptitude would no longer be visited solely on the victim. Strenuous efforts were made to develop new and expand older philanthropic organizations to cope with some of the urgent needs that fell between government and business.

The momentum for social welfare and humanitarian reform came from a great many sources and was reenforced by a great many institutions. Among the most important was the trade union, for, by its very nature, it was primarily concerned with improving the conditions of work and life for its membership. In pursuing its primary aims, it followed a broad approach, since labor leaders had recognized that the quality of a man's life, while dependent on his having a job and income, involved much more—his political status, his educational opportunities, his dignity as a human being.

The broad approach of trade unions helps to explain the types of cases which comprise this chapter. They have been subsumed under the title of human dignity, but they are concerned specifically with the extent to which considerations of both physical and psychological health, integrity, and personal freedom must be weighed in assessing the performance of a workingman both on and off the job.

One important factor undoubtedly has contributed significantly to making the community, and therefore the arbitrator, aware of such elements when conflicts arise between an employer and the union in the interpretation of a collective bargaining agreement. How one thinks about human beings—and their problems and potentialities—depends not only on the progress that a society has made on the moral front but also on its comprehension of the nature of human beings and the environment in which they live and work. Advancing the frontiers of knowledge thus becomes a dynamic factor in altering the established framework with its conventional distinctions between right and wrong. This is clearly illustrated by the cases which involve a consideration of the extent to which a worker's emotional state has relevance to evaluating his work performance. An outstanding illustration of the interrelation between new knowledge and new patterns of discipline was the experience of the armed forces of the United States during World War II.

Increasingly, poor health has become the most acceptable explanation for poor performance in our society. We assume that the condition of a person's health lies outside his control; that, in the presence of severe disability, an individual cannot properly draw upon his full resources; and that, even if he could, it would be wrong to request him to, for the strain might result in permanent damage, whereas rest or light work might be the quickest and the best way for him to make a complete recovery. But few people are always in the best of health. And since an employer pays people to perform their assigned functions during a prescribed time, there is considerable cause for conflict. First, our society has come to believe the sick man is entitled to consideration; and, second, the exigencies of the work place are such that multiple claims of illness can quickly prove disruptive.

The case of an employee of eleven years' service at the St. Joseph's Lead Company illuminates the conflicts that can so easily arise on this front. Arnold Thornborrow claimed that he requested light work on the night that a conveyor belt broke down because he had had a fainting spell earlier that day. He knew he had high blood pressure. During the course of his shift, the foreman to whom he had originally made the request had left and a new foreman asked Thornborrow to bring a block and tackle to help repair the belt. Since the repair work would have involved a considerable amount of climbing, Thornborrow decided that he would leave rather than follow the foreman's orders. The following day he reported to the company physician who found that his blood pressure was high. Nevertheless, his foreman told him to take five days off, since he had been previously advised by the physician that Thornborrow could "do any work that you have for him."

The foreman testified that he had given Thornborrow the penalty of a layoff because Thornborrow "was mad and not for being or playing sick." The arbitrator held that a worker should accept an assignment and then grieve, but that an employee is entitled to "refuse a work assignment which he believes will be dangerous to his life, limbs, or health *unless* he is regularly engaged in a pursuit which such risks are normally incident thereto."If he should avail himself of "on the spot" privileges then the burden of proof is on the employee. The arbitrator contended that while such a privilege holds a threat to the orderly operation of a plant, it is hemmed in with sufficient procedural safeguards that it can not be readily abused. After all, the burden of the proof rested with the worker. The arbitrator lifted the penalty.

A similar case was presented by the conflict at Western Insulated Wire Company. Tom Anguello, a coiler in the shipping room, was asked to bale some scrap wire that had been brought in. Although he had claimed no disability when hired, Anguello, who had a history of asthma, was assigned to coiling after he found a waxer's job too dusty. Every few weeks, scrap is baled and the usual practice is to assign one of the coilers to help. Sometimes, even foremen lend a hand. Anguello had always declined this work and had been excused. This time he said "No, the job is dirty." The arbitrator allowed that the foreman might not have known of Anguello's asthma and may have misinterpreted the answer to mean that he was unwilling to do his share of "dirty work." After the personnel officer talked to Anguello, who kept repeating, "I can't," the foreman was permitted to discharge him. Said the arbitrator: "It is established practice to recognize . . . a health danger as an adequate excuse for discharging an otherwise valid order of management, *especially* where, as here, no real inconvenience could be occasioned to management by accepting it." It appeared to the arbitrator that management was "forcing an issue" at the risk of sacrificing the right of a valued employee.

In a group of cases involving epileptic seizures, management will usually be upheld if, before discharging a worker, it makes a conscientious effort to find him an assignment where his seizures will not jeopardize others and will not lead to costly errors. On the other hand, arbitrators are reluctant to uphold a discharge for such cause if management responds to a seizure with immediate dismissal without making any effort at reassignment. An interesting illustration of how advances in medicine must be taken into account is the striking progress that has been made in controlling seizures through new drugs.

Management has long been plagued by excessive absenteeism on days preceding and following holidays or weekends. It consequently makes special efforts to enforce attendance on these days. In the following case, management realized that an employee who was sick or injured, and could present evidence to prove it, could not be punished for such an absence. The conflict arose as to whether a woman employee who stayed away from work on Friday because a stove exploded in her home the night before had an excusable absence on the ground that she had suffered from shock. The employee argued that she was "too nervous to work" but the company claimed that she stayed home to clean up the mess. The arbitrator allowed that she had suffered no physical injury but that the resulting "shock was an effect on her person." The line between emotional disturbance and poor motivation is a narrow one, but, as the Army discovered in World War II, every effort must be made to recognize it, or else injustice can result. In this case, the arbitrator was willing, on the evidence, to give the employee the benefit of the doubt and to hold that she may have been too upset to perform effectively on her job.

Psychological factors may even be brought into play when there is a major and uncontested breach of discipline. This occurred at Swift and Company when Benson Walker, an employee with 25 years' service, struck his foreman. Almost every contract provides for discharge in the event of physical altercation, especially if it is directed by an employee toward his supervisor. And, yet, the arbitrator gave sufficient weight to the mitigating circumstances, which, in this case, related to the employee's emotional state, to reduce the stipulated penalty. The facts are simple. Walker had recently been transferred to a new department and was apparently under some strain. He believed that the foreman was "riding" him and was unduly critical of his work. There was illness in his family and he had been denied time off when he requested it to recover from a nervous upset. On the day of the episode, the worker who was helping him on his new job was out. The altercation arose when the foreman asked Walker when he was going to get the truck unloaded. He replied that he was working as quickly as possible. The foreman went up to him and told him to go to the office. "At this point Walker struck the foreman and as the foreman got off the truck Walker kicked him and then followed the foreman and continued to kick and strike at him."

The union admitted that "a case of this sort ordinarily would not be brought to arbitration since it is recognized that striking a foreman or fellow worker is intolerable." In the arbitrator's words, such conduct, if condoned by management, "would result in the complete destruction of morale within the plant."

The union brought the action because it believed the pun-

ishment to be too severe in light of the difficulties under which
Walker was laboring. As proof of his good and non-violent character, it brought into evidence the fact that he served as min-
ister of the Zion Chapel in Chicago.

The arbitrator agreed that once just cause for discharge had
been established, Walker's long service with the company had
little bearing. Yet, he was struck with the fact that "the out-
burst was probably as strange and shocking to Walker as it was
to the supervisor." He went on to conclude that "an employee
who had proved his worth for many years fell victim to circumstances which were partly beyond his control." On the basis
of these "circumstances," he directed the company to reinstate
the worker without retroactive pay.

The company chafed under the decision and six months later
asked for a rehearing. It argued that "sympathy with the worker
was beyond the scope of the arbitrator's discretion. The company
felt that the award might encourage other employees in acts of
this type . . . if they can supply some sort of Freudian alibi."
The arbitrator held, however, that in a quasi-judicial process
such as arbitration, there is room for mercy and sympathy in
reaching a decision of a "just finding." He considered the company's fears of a rampant Freudianism unwarranted. And, on
the crucial issue as to whether he had substituted his judgment
for that of the plant's superintendent, he acknowledged that this
might happen now and then "as a natural part of the judicial
process."

There were fewer problems and less disagreement when the
Board of Arbitrators at the Curtiss Wright Plant in Columbus,
Ohio, decided to countermand the discharge of Thorpe, a tool-
worker who had been separated from the payroll after three
incidents of poor work and incompetence. The board, in reaching its decision, concluded that Thorpe, who had been retained

then, that a man cannot be required to waive basic rights in order to protect his job.

Jim Crandall was discharged from the aluminum sash department of Trimm Industries of Los Angeles for failure to meet the production quota after he had received two warnings. In seeking to reverse management's decision, the union had argued that Crandall took great pride in his work, that he did not avoid the more difficult windows in selecting those he would work on, and that his efforts should be assessed not by reference to an assembly line quota but in terms of individualized work. The company acknowledged that Crandall was a good worker and pointed to the fact that it had long tolerated his low output because of his craftsmanship. It said, however, that it could not afford to keep a man who could only do experimental work, "for no company can stay in business unless they can produce at a cost which will allow them to sell at a profit." The arbitrator upheld the company. With respect to the union's emphasis on Crandall's "instinct of workmanship," the arbitrator had this to say: "If as the union contends, Crandall deliberately selected the difficult work jobs out of pride of workmanship or permitted others to leave him difficult jobs, he has only himself to blame for the consequences." Employers are in business to make a profit, not to create opportunities for workmen to exercise their instincts of workmanship. If a man is only concerned with the exercise of his skills, he must go into business for himself and assume the risk of making or losing money.

Among the risks that management seeks to minimize are those resulting from theft. This is not the type of misdemeanor where penalties less severe than discharge should first be employed. "Theft," said the arbitrator in a case involving the Moline Works of International Harvester Company, "is intrinsically so serious an offense that management cannot properly be required—as a matter of contract obligation—to run the risk of its repetition." A worker was caught trying to remove from the plant three pieces of steel which he had sheared, drilled, and welded together to form a hitch for a trailer he was building. When caught, he had lied in saying that he had taken the metal from among the products of a regular shearing operation.

Despite his knowledge that the contract was clear and that management had acted within its rights, the arbitrator decided to discuss the other "side of this case." He stated that, in his view, to stamp a man as a "thief" merely because he had made a trailer hitch out of a few cents' worth of steel would be a shame. The grievant may be a fool to have risked so much for so little. He may be a weak man, since he lied when he was caught. But, the arbitrator contended, it would be both cruel and wrong to deprive him of his job and jeopardize his future because of this. "Supervision clearly knew what the grievant was doing. It could have stopped him—warned him—and thereby save an employee. It did not *have* to do so. But its failure to do so, its emphasis on *catching* him rather than preventing him should give management considerable food for thought." The arbitrator made a recommendation to put him back to work; he has had his lesson. Management has an obligation not only to salvage materials but to salvage a human being.

The last case involving the dignity of the worker as a human being grew out of the conditions incident to the reinstatement of a group of five workers at the Central Franklin Process Company. The men had been suspended because of an altercation with the foreman which occurred away from the plant premises when the men told him that they did not like him and did not consider his treatment of them to be fair. The evidence is unclear whether abusive language or threats actually were employed or whether the foreman's car actually was blocked. The company did not discuss the case with the union committee and it stipulated that the men could get their jobs back only after they had apologized to their foreman. The arbitrator upheld the suspension but not the extraction of an apology. "The men were being asked to say that they were sorry for something that they may have thought was justified." The arbitrator pointed out that to insist upon their apologizing as a condition of their reemployment was forcing them "to eat crow." The arbitrator was not so much bothered by the company's expecting an apology but by its exacting it without having given the men a chance to tell their story. Once again, we see that power must not be used to humble men, for the protection of a man's pride takes precedence over the maintenance of plant efficiency.

The last set of cases involves considerations of freedom. How far does the employer's authority stretch in a society that by tradition and law is strongly committed to pluralistic power centers? Where does the public authority of the civil courts begin and end? And what are the limits within which management's private rights can be exercised? Or, to note another shady area, what are the rights and obligations of an individual under an employment contract and how are these to be squared with his basic civil rights? The following cases bring these conflict areas into purview and indicate how the arbitrators have dealt with them.

Many issues were involved in the strike precipitated at the Univis Lens Company at its Dayton, Ohio, plant. Two unions had been attempting for some time to be recognized as the bargaining agent; the one that had won by a bare margin a year or two before was locked in a dispute with management which led the losing union to petition its opponents' decertification by the National Labor Relations Board. Feeling was running very high and all the prerequisites for violence were present when the plant was struck. The local police were unable to cope with the crowd at the plant gate. The National Guard was called out. Finally, an agreement was reached which included a provision to arbitrate the discharge of ten workers whom the company did not reemploy because of improper activities during the strike despite its "forget and forgive policy."

The arbitrator said there was no "flat yes or no answer to the question of whether an employer is entitled to discipline employees for improper action committed during a strike which does not violate the contract." Second, he held that the company was not free to pick ten out of a much larger group of workers who had defied the court order and engaged in mass picketing. Finally, he held that the case of each individual must be taken up separately to consider whether the worker had committed physical violence. He found that Marilyn Hasselbeck had sprayed "skunk oil" on supervisory personnel, and that Bill Steinmetz, Jr., had thrown a stinkbomb into the plant in addition to kicking and striking people. These were acts of hoodlumism and "just cause" for discharge. But Martha Woodie, however, had done nothing more than many others who had not been discharged and, therefore, just cause for dismissal could not be found in her case. And, in this manner, the arbitrator continued to carefully assess each case. He then came to the nub of the conflict as it affects freedom in a pluralistic society; "Whatever punishment the Court decides to mete out on those who violated its order must be left with the Court. The company is not a law-enforcing agency, the attitude of the Dayton civil authorities notwithstanding."

Management may not even use proof of civil crime as cause to terminate employment unless the company can prove that it will be vulnerable if it continues the employment of the worker. The Martin Oil Company discharged Mr. M. because he had shot his wife; the company contended that this action revealed "traits in Mr. M.'s personality which make it highly inadvisable for the company to retain him as a gasoline truck driver. Mr. M's action has shown that he has an unstable temperament and that his continued employment as a driver would expose the company to the risk of accident and suit for personal damages as well as the danger of loss of customers through possible inconsiderate action on his part. . . . What Mr. M. did is known to fellow employees and to customers. This fact alone would make it impossible to maintain easy harmonious relationship."

The arbitrator reviewed the facts of the case and accepted the probability that the head wound inflicted upon the wife had been the result of an accident. He concluded that Mr. M. had been foolhardy to brandish a weapon but decided that there was no proof that he did so in passion and intended to kill his wife or that he lacked self-control. The arbitrator was impressed that Mr. M. had driven for nineteen years and had never before given evidence of ungovernable temper or emotional instability. He was most impressed with the fact that Mrs. M. was not sufficiently frightened to press any charges. "If Mr. M. has lost his acceptability to customers that fact . . . will quickly appear and the company will have concrete evidence, rather than speculation on which to base its decision." Mr. M. was reinstated. The courts of the land have one jurisdiction; management, another. The two should be kept apart. The arbitrator held that there is little gained and much lost by the intermingling of the two.

Nevertheless, public and private power do become so intertwined at times that it appears best not to try to wrench them apart because the loss may be greater than the gain. That appears to have been the conclusion of the arbitrator who upheld the Wolverine Shoe and Tanning Corporation when it disciplined Jim Calvetti for failing to observe its rule that no employee could park on the street on which the plant was located. The rule had been established to avoid possible danger to other employees who are picked up after hours and to make it easier for salesmen who carry heavy bags. Calvetti argued that the company had usurped rights in its making a public street out of bounds for workers' parking and further that this was interference with workers outside of the plant. The arbitrator denied the latter contention explicitly and evaded the former. The fact that the grievant was the union president meant that he knew that in the event of a disagreement he should obey first and then grieve. Although he was definitely in the wrong in his "itching" to challenge the company, the arbitrator found discharge too severe a penalty and ordered that it be rescinded. The arbitrator was impressed with, even if he disapproved of, the methods that Calvetti used to test his rights of citizenship.

One of the hallmarks of a democracy is that the area of private choice be as broad as possible, especially when the action involved has no untoward effect on other members of the community. For this reason, there is little if any attempt on the part of employers to interfere in the social or sexual behavior of adults. Yet, the Braniff Airways was upheld when it disciplined a captain by demoting him for a period of months because he acknowledged breaking a company rule which stipulated that "if you or any other married member of our flight crew group dates our hostesses or becomes involved in any form of 'back door' romance with them that results in any criticisms of yourselves or the company, you will be subject to immediate discharge." The arbitrator found that because of "the peculiar nature and quality of the relations of hostesses with the company, the public, and the safety and comfort of passengers in flight . . . the company should have the right to establish regulations with the powers of enforcement." In his opinion, he also called attention to generally recognized and accepted social conventions. The company instituted a rule justified by the nature of its business that was in harmony, not in dissonance, with prevailing attitudes. That such a rule might limit the freedom of pilots and hostesses was not relevant since the action involved might cause disturbance both to the efficient operation of an airliner and the harmony of family life.

Revelations of improper behavior between pilots and hostesses while airlines were in flight were made public in 1962 in connection with hearings growing out of the struggle of the flight engineers to protect their jobs. Arbitrators, it appears, have done their best to widen consideration for human dignity in the realm of employment, but this does not include support of personal freedom when it jeopardizes not only the efficiency of the company but the safety of its customers.

PART FOUR

TOWARD A NEW BALANCE

10. The Scope of Managerial Rights

While the roots of industrial arbitration can be traced back to the last century, its large-scale growth and development took place during the last quarter-century. This latter period has been characterized by a great number of major changes in the structure and functioning of the American economy; it encompassed the legislation of the New Deal, the conflicts of World War II and Korea, the penetration of government into the nation's economic life through defense and space expenditures. It was a period of large gains in output, somewhat smaller gains in employment, and a profit record which has been, especially in recent years, spotty and even a little disappointing. On balance, it was a period of progress, almost uninterrupted progress except for minor cyclical reversals.

Nevertheless, there were a number of disturbing developments so that the leaders of American industry have not been completely confident about the direction of the economy or the future of their own enterprises. During the past several years, this restiveness has been on the increase. Despite President Eisenhower's conservatism, the federal budget continued to increase rapidly and the power of labor was not substantially changed from what it had been during the preceding administration. For the first time in a great many years the future of the dollar has been called into question. The recovery of Western Europe and Japan has proceeded so rapidly that many American industries now confront increasingly severe competition

from abroad. Additional disturbing trends could be identified:
the ability of the Russians to unsettle various international
markets; the unremitting pressure on the United States to continue large foreign aid programs; the whipsaw in which the
federal government is caught between maintaining high tax
rates or tolerating large budget deficits; the mounting diseconomies of growth represented by the ever-larger backlog of un-
solved urban problems.

In the present context, it is necessary to precipitate only two
findings from this review: a great number of significant changes
have been occurring in the structure and functioning of the
American economy during the last quarter century and business
leaders manifest a substantial degree of uneasiness and dis-
quietude about the implications of these changes for the future
well-being of their enterprises and for the larger economy and
society. The American economy has long been characterized
by far-reaching technological and market alterations and business itself has been, and continues to be, largely responsible for
such transformations. Hence, the mounting anxiety of the business community that something may be askew is derived from
its belief that qualitative adjustments are occurring in the essential mechanisms of a competitive economy. Since they believe
that the strength and survival of the free enterprise system, as
they have known it, is the *sine qua non* for continued national
progress, they are disturbed by various trends which appear to
be resulting in fundamental changes in their authority and latitude to manage their businesses effectively.

When a great many parts of a complex system are undergoing change and when the consequences of such change are
viewed with suspicion, it is inevitable that those who are disturbed by the drift of events will single out for special condem-
nation one or another of the multiple forces that are operating

on the system. In a democratic society, discussion and argument themselves are important levers for stability or change and protagonists often seek to buttress a particular position by recourse to theories and facts which hold promise of support.

Disturbed as they are by a great many contemporary developments, many American business leaders have singled out as a major cause of their difficulties the circumscriptions, limitations, and reductions in their authority to manage their own businesses. They are not interested in a careful review of the major reasons for such a development for they are participants, not philosophers: their definition of the situation is determined by their values and goals. The nature of their education and their work also helps to explain their reactions to the challenge; they seek the assistance of others to stem the drift which they consider fraught with danger not only to business but to the future of society as well.

These businessmen believe that the recent developments are in fundamental conflict with our history, values, and position. They recall that this nation was constructed on the principle of reserving for the individual the maximum amount of freedom to decide how he wanted to live and what he wanted to do with what he owned. Only a limited number of powers were allocated to government—local, state, or federal. The founding fathers, despite some differences of opinion among them, were of one mind when it came to fundamentals—the best guarantee of freedom was the retention by the individual of the broadest possible scope for decision-making. And early in the nation's history, when the Supreme Court decided that the corporation possessed many of the same rights as individuals, continuity was maintained in basic structure; the corporate owner as well as the individual had wide scope for decision-making. In recent decades, another extension of this trend became manifest. The agents of owners—the managers—were able to subsume for themselves the authorities inherent in ownership. The historical record, then, is clear. The right to do what one likes with his property lies at the very foundation of our historical experience. This is a basis for management's growing concern with the restrictions and limitations which have increasingly come to characterize an arena where the widest scope for individual initiative previously prevailed.

What additional dimensions are uncovered if attention is focused on considerations growing out of more recent interactions between political democracy and a competitive economy? Do they further reenforce management's growing concern with the loss of its rights? In the United States a sound democracy has gone hand in hand with a free economy—one in which there has been a wide diffusion of economic power. But an economy predicated on individuals pursuing their own interests has had to rely on a competitive mechanism to bring about a sound allocation of scarce resources and an equitable distribution of rewards. At least, such has been the prevailing ideology no matter how often and how strenuously business has acted to moderate the untoward influences of rampant competition. Management is therefore increasingly disturbed when it finds itself forced to operate more and more under restraints which limit its ability to pursue its self-interest as aggressively and persistently as the value premises of the society have long supported. Of course production can be secured under other systems in which centralized controls play a dominant role. But management contends that a democratic society cannot long flourish if there is a concentration of economic power and control under governmental aegis. Management fears that the current restrictions under which it is forced to operate will increase and multiply until the basic economic principles on which this democracy has been predicated become eroded. The fear is that the already established reductions in its authority and the threat of further losses in the years ahead will inevitably lower the productivity of the economy. Our economy relies on individual initiative; if management is hobbled and restricted in its search for profits then the performance of the system will inevitably worsen.

In addition to the arguments that it has mustered from history and from the value orientations of our free-enterprise democratic system, management has had recourse to organizational realities in its efforts to protect its rights. It has argued with great emphasis that a corporation is not a club and cannot be run on a democratic basis. The competitive market is a severe taskmaster. Management has contended that such a market has no tolerance for the slow or the sluggish. Its rewards are reserved for those who know what to do and when to do it and who succeed in taking advantage of every opportunity. Only an enterprise which is so organized that it can plan ahead, and which can shift tack with every change in the market, has prospect of making money. Now, of course, not everybody can be engaged in basic policy decisions. This must be reserved for a limited number of executives whose function is to plan, direct, and control the work of others. Hence, even if we were to disregard our history and our values or even if we were willing to tolerate centralized instead of decentralized power in the political and economic realm, it is argued, it would still be necessary for the management of large organizations engaged in the production and distribution of goods to exercise wide decision-making powers. For no large organization can run itself. It must be managed if it is to perform effectively. Herein lies the basic rationale for underpinning managerial prerogatives and rights.

Leaders of business have buttressed their argument by the

lessons of history, the basic value commitments of the nation, and the logic of organization. As long as the country does not turn its back on democracy or on free enterprise, it must support the rights of management to manage. They contend that many errors have been made in the recent past—errors that should be corrected at the earliest possible time. But even more important, all who are concerned about economic freedom and social progress must insure that they do not add to the mistakes and errors of the recent past. Even if recent history cannot be undone, we must not compound the faulty analyses and discussions which have already stripped management of many of its basic rights.

On the face of it, employers appear to have good reason to be concerned about recent trends. Even if, in their counter-attack, they occasionally engage in overstatement and distortion, they are justified in being disturbed about the status of their rights to manage their business as they see fit.

Recourse to first principles is always desirable but it may not by itself clarify the full range of issues involved in a conflict. Moreover, since the contestants may have recourse to different principles or draw different inferences from the same principles the conflict may become deepened rather than compromised or resolved. It may therefore be helpful to review the major developments that have taken place in delineating the rights of management as they bump into the rights of workers and the changing values of the society as reflected in arbitration decisions.

Changes in this particular arena are but one segment of changes that are going on throughout the economy and society and which are affecting to some degree the rights of management. When the courts prohibit certain types of mergers; when Congress or a state legislature levy business taxes; when unions develop sufficient power to insist on pension plans and supplementary unemployment insurance; when an aroused group of Negro customers decide to boycott the products of a firm that has a discriminatory employment policy, when any of these actions—or any of a hundred related types of action—takes place, management is affected. But, here, we are concerned solely with the impact on the rights of management that grow out of the decisions rendered by arbitrators as a result of procedures established for the settlement of grievances under collective bargaining.

In terms of the preceding chapters, the crucial rights likely to be affected are those related to the decision-making powers of management to determine where to locate its plants and what to produce, its margin of freedom to introduce changes in the productive process, the scope available to it to set forth the conditions under which individuals and groups perform their work. It is along these major axes that managerial decision-making power will be reviewed and assessed. The basic question that must be raised and answered with respect to each of these conflict areas is what has in fact happened by way of circumscribing management's rights and what can we deduce to be the importance of the restrictions.

On the crucial question of location and relocation, the highest court of the land has only recently (1962) upheld the new doctrine that an employer is bound under a broad collective bargaining agreement to honor the seniority of workers if a plant is dismembered and a new one erected, possibly thousands of miles away. But the full sweep of this new doctrine will only be revealed with time. No arbitrator or court has held that an employer is not free to relocate except where he has explicitly bound himself not to do so, or to do so only after consultation with the union. Nothing has so far transpired nor does anything loom on the horizon which is likely to prohibit the continuing exercise of the managerial right to determine where to locate or relocate. The basic issue about which conflict rages is whether the employer who relocates is under an obligation to workers who have served him faithfully for many years. There are many contracts that management enters into that severely limit its future scope of action. It would never assume that it should be, much less does it seek to become free of these obligations. But in the case of agreements with a union, it enters them reluctantly; limits them severely; and hopes that its obligations under them will terminate sooner rather than later.

On this issue of relocation, the signs do point to a broadening of the employer's responsibility. Arbitrators and judges alike have begun to hold that employers cannot discharge without further consideration men whose entire working lives—their energies, their skills, their loyalties—have been devoted to a particular enterprise. These decisions reflect action already taken by many employers, union and non-union alike, irrespective of the existence of a labor agreement. Many large corporate enterprises have recognized an obligation to their employees when they close down operations in one locale and expand them elsewhere. In many instances, they not only provide a comparable job in the new location for those who want to transfer but they are likely to encourage them to relocate by paying their traveling expenses and facilitating the sale of their house and the purchase of a new one. To those who do not want to move a responsible corporation is likely to provide separation allowances based on years of service, and for long-time workers this can reach substantial sums.

The nub of the recent arbitration awards and court decisions is an effort to institutionalize this obligation which many managements have in the past freely taken on. To an older worker, the costs of a plant shutdown are among the most serious of all risks that he confronts. While the union negotiates for him always for a limited number of years, a major concern of most workers is their continuing job security. In the absence of some restraint on the employer to relocate, the worker's rights slowly acquired through a series of collective bargaining agreements can be completely destroyed.

Over the decades, management has been forced by governmental legislation and by trade union pressure to budget for many costs previously borne exclusively by the worker—unemployment, accident and illness, retirement. Recent decisions to protect seniority in a new locality is less of a limitation of management's right to manage than these earlier developments, which forced management to absorb many new costs. Recent arbitration decisions, then, do not interfere with management's right to locate or relocate where it desires—where it will be most profitable *as long as* management takes into account and makes provisions for workers who have acquired seniority. The new pressures on management are nothing more nor less than a requirement to discharge the obligations which it has assumed by entering into a series of contractual agreements with its workers.

There are many parallels between the recent decisons about location and those bearing on specialization, which most frequently find expression through the adjudication of conflicts which arise out of subcontracting. Here too the issue is not whether management may or may not subcontract. The issue is whether, in seeking to subcontract, it will significantly damage the rights of workers which accrue to them under an agreement. Time and time again, arbitrators have upheld the right of management to subcontract if changes have occurred in the

structure or functioning of the business that make it more efficient and economical for an employer to buy on the outside
goods or services which it had previously supplied.

Arbitrators have interfered with management's move to subcontract first, when they conclude that the move is a devious
device which will weaken or destroy the bargaining unit with
which management had earlier entered into an agreement. Or
they interdict the free exercise of management's rights if in the
exercise of these rights,—the rights of workers—to work, to overtime, or to income (all guaranteed by the agreement)—will be
jeopardized. The arbitrators also refused to accept lowest dollar
cost for getting work completed as an overriding criterion. While
arbitrators realize that a firm must remain competitive in order
to survive, they will not agree to lower costs as the sole criterion.
Arbitrators know that frequently employers operate within narrow margins. And while they are inclined to support management when it can prove major financial gains from subcontracting or major losses from failure to subcontract, they tend to
deny managerial action that will take work away from workers.

On the other hand, they are likely to uphold management's
rights to subcontract if the company does not have the equipment needed to get the job done efficiently, if its workers do
not possess the requisite skills, or if time is a pressing consideration. While management continues to retain wide scope to contract out, its scope under collective bargaining is not unlimited.
It cannot sub-contract solely because it can get work done more
cheaply, especially if the only difference between performing
the work on its own account and outside are the applicable
wage rates.

Despite parallels between the problems raised by relocation
and subcontracting, there is one important difference. When a
plant shuts down and relocates, the employees who do not move

are deprived of work. Subcontracting usually reflects a more fluid situation. Collective bargaining agreements run for a limited number of years. Local employment conditions may change quite radically during the course of a specific agreement and particularly over several agreements. Sometimes, there is more than enough work for the groups covered by the agreement and it is not difficult for management to get their consent to subcontract. At other times, there may be many workers either on short time or unemployed waiting to be recalled. The union's attitude to subcontracting will depend on the labor market. Moreover, the arbitrator will attempt to assess not only the employment repercussions but the short and long run considerations of efficiency and financial return to the enterprise.

But once again we cannot say that a basic management right has been eroded because employers do not possess the unilateral right to subcontract. As every student of the American economy knows, subcontracting is a basic facet of contemporary business practice. It has been on the increase in recent years under the twin pressures of complex defense contracts and managerial reassessment of the inherent limitations of vertical integration. As the old economists warned, there is a specialized component to management and it does not follow therefore that a company because it is successful in one area will necessarily be successful if it broadens and deepens the scope of its activities. Since defense contracts have to be completed as quickly as possible, another potent factor has been added to expand subcontracting. The prime contractor simply cannot meet the rigid deadlines without securing outside help.

Recently, still another factor has become important. Many employers, seeking to escape from being victimized by jurisdictional struggles between members of the same or different unions have sought to contract out their maintenance work.

Some have found this satisfactory; others have found that they did not really free themselves from intra- or inter-union rivalry but simply traded one type of conflict for another; and still others found that for technical reasons subcontracting did not adequately meet their needs.

It would be very difficult to develop a meaningful index of the extent of subcontracting today as compared to some earlier time. But this much is clear: subcontracting remains sufficiently pervasive to throw serious doubt on the contention that recent limitations on subcontracting are still one more piece of evidence of the erosion of managerial rights. What is involved in the conflicts over subcontracting is the care that management must take and the costs that it must assume in exercising its rights in the face of rights that the agreement has granted the workers.

The second major area of conflict relates to the scope of managerial decision-making with respect to the many different aspects involved in the introduction of new machinery and the different use of existing machinery where such changes carry alterations in the work conventionally performed by one or another group of employees. For example, the affected workers may find themselves out of a job; they may find that their old skill is no longer required and that they must be retrained; they may find the new work conditions less favorable; finally, some workers may actually be confronted with a reduction in weekly or annual earnings. These are but some of the important impacts of technological change on the workingman. The arbitrator is likely, therefore, to move circumspectly in defining what management may and may not do during the life of a contract, which after all establishes the terms of employment between workers and management.

There are certain propositions that can help to frame the

problem. On the one hand, American industry has long enjoyed a significant technological lead over other advanced economies. Such a position could have been achieved and maintained only under conditions that did not prevent management from exploiting new machinery and new processes. At least, American management could not have been under any differential disadvantage in this regard. On the other hand, there has been repeated evidence in recent years—in printing, stevedoring, railroading, airlines, and many other sectors of the economy—of the serious difficulties that management confronts when it seeks to exploit fully the potentialities inherent in the new technology in their industry. The difficulties reflect more often than not a rigidity on the part of management to buy back work rules to which it earlier agreed; or to provide some reasonable quid pro quo for the severe consequences that the new machinery will have on the jobs of many workers. The rapid mechanization of bituminous coal mining and the recent contract on the West Coast in stevedoring are proof of the inherent elasticity that continues to exist for an imaginative management.

A basic principle appears to run through most of the recent arbitration awards. Management's right to avail itself of new and improved machinery, to install it, and to make necessary adjustments in work assignments is overwhelmingly upheld. The unions submit few challenges to this basic management right. Labor has not generally attempted to bar American management from moving ahead in introducing ever more modern equipment and to develop more efficient methods of production. The substantial decline in employment in railroading, in steel, and in many other sectors of the economy during the past decade is proof of the continuing scope for management to introduce machines which eliminate jobs. A single fact can make clear the potency of continuing technological innovation. In the past decade, employment in the manufacturing sector declined from about 17.5 million workers to 16.5 million with a more than 25 percent increase in output.

What then are the issues over which conflict erupts? The first relates to whether the changes in work assignment that management desires to introduce are in fact the direct consequence of a change in technology. Is there a basis for management's upsetting the conditions agreed to when the contract was signed? Without substantial reasons, management is not entitled to alter unilaterally the terms of the employment contract. The introduction of new technology is usually considered a just reason. Hence, one type of basic conflict in this arena relates to the substantive determination of whether in fact a real technological change has been introduced which necessitates changes in the employment pattern. The arbitrator seldom protects a worker against a true technological change. Moreover, few unions would even attempt to have men continued in jobs where their skills have been made redundant by the introduction of a new machine unless management had earlier agreed by contract to their retention.

But, of course, the unions do have a major interest in any changes which threaten the jobs or earnings of their members. While management can introduce a new machine, the union is very much on the alert to see that management takes all reasonable steps to protect the seniority of workers who may be adversely affected—the setting of new rates and other facets of the employment situation. A striking difference between American and British trade unions is the emphasis that American trade unions have placed on seniority. In a rapidly growing economy, protection for the older members has enabled most unions and the society at large to be less concerned about the effects of technological change. If the adverse effect of these changes is limited primarily to workers who only recently were added to the payroll, their displacement is a price that the union is willing to accept in order to insure that the company remains vital and profitable and the jobs of the more senior workers thereby be made more secure. In Great Britain, the absence of job security has led to a much greater concern of the unions toward technological innnovation. The contemporary American scene is more confused since manufacturing employment has been declining, not growing, during the past decade and continual improvements in technology in such major industries as automobiles and steel have begun to affect adversely workers with ten, fifteen, and even twenty years' seniority.

To return to the specific conflict which arises between management and labor as a result of technological change: arbitrators usually insist that in exercising its right to improve its operations through the introduction of new technology, management has an obligation to find, if possible, alternative employment for senior workers who have been caught by the change. Here is another facet of the broad framework that was earlier identified with respect to management's rights to relocate and subcontract: a collective bargaining agreement has, as a major objective, the protection of seniority. Management must therefore consider the impact of each of its efforts to achieve greater efficiency to be sure that the valuable equities of workers guaranteed them under the contract are disturbed as little as possible.

The issue of work rules which was catapulted to the fore by management and which led to the long steel strike of 1959 brings still another aspect of this problem into perspective. For the sake of simplicity, work rules can be defined here as local practices under which work is conducted which, through earlier explicit or, more typically, implicit agreement, have become accepted by both management and labor. Workers—and first line supervisors, too—have a deep interest in and place high value on established practices and routines which determine how work is carried on—what management can require workers to do and what it cannot require them to do. Over time, a great many specific adjustments and readjustments are likely to be accepted by both—many having been initiated by management. The aim of most work rules, when first introduced, is to lead to some change which will contribute to the more effective utilization of the work force for which labor will receive some consideration. With the passage of time and in the face of many technological, organizational, and other alterations, some of these previously accepted rules will prove to be a deterrent to efficiency.

It should be noted, however, that these practices are not instituted unilaterally. Either management or the workers request a change and the other obtains a concession in return. While management can often present to the public some extreme examples of work practices which on the face of them have no conceivable relation to the rational organization of the work process, such examples are not common. But the crucial issue is that these practices are valued by workers who feel that they have earned them through earlier concessions. The real challenge to management is to calculate the probable cost of the rule and to explore whether it cannot bargain or buy its way out of an arrangement which earlier was satisfactory to both parties.

When, therefore, management seeks to disregard or alter an accepted practice in order to reduce costs and where it seeks to do so without the umbrella of a technological innnovation or some other valid reason for changing practices, its effort will usually be challenged by the union. And the challenge will frequently be upheld by the arbitrator. For, in the opinion of most arbitrators, this is not a proper exercise of managerial initiative but is often a unilateral change of the terms of employment.

The foregoing analysis does not imply either that management is unable to change any work rule, or, that in the event that a technological change has been introduced, it has complete freedom of action. Neither is correct. When management can prove to the satisfaction of the arbitrator that it is engaged in a significant alteration in the carrying out of a major operation, such as maintenance or warehousing, and that significant efficiencies can be obtained by altering the work process, and if further, the arbitrator finds no serious jeopardy to the jobs or income of the employees in such a change he is likely to permit the management to disregard established work rules. Managerial initiative which seeks company gains by economizing in the use of labor will usually be upheld as long as the arbitrator has assured himself that important equities guaranteed to the workers under the agreement will not thereby be jeopardized.

The introduction of a new machine provides no umbrella for management to take unilateral actions for instance to determine work loads and pay on the new jobs. Management has the right to establish new standards in accordance with the principles expressed or implied in the agreement, but it is unlikely that the arbitrator will uphold them unless the company has proceeded in an objective manner. Many cases have been brought to arbitration because time studies were carried out without consideration of all the relevant factors. In many instances the arbitrator has supported the union's contention that since there are no objective standards to judge equitable work rates these should be bargained.

We see then that in recent years the pressure that unions have been able to exert through agreements as interpreted by arbitrators in the crucial areas of managerial decision-making—relocation, subcontracting, technological improvements, and work rules—has resulted in increasingly hobbling management. Some claim that it is no longer possible for management to discharge effectively its basic functions of managing because its long established rights to exercise control over its expenditures or its work organization have been restricted, limited, and hedged.

It is true that management cannot move as freely today as in former years, to exploit changes in the market, in technology, or in the art of management itself. But there are a great many variables affecting management, almost all of them in flux, and one cannot, therefore, select just one or two for appraisal and derive conclusions solely from them.

What are some of the determinants in the larger economy that impinge on the union's efforts to influence the scope and direction of managerial behavior with respect to location, subcontracting, and changes in the organization of the work?

The contemporary economy is characterized by the expansion of the multi-plant corporation; the mobility of the population enhanced by a relative decline in the costs of transportation; the shift in the location of industry from primary consideration of natural resources to dependence on human resources; the aggressive actions of local government in underdeveloped, manpower surplus areas to secure new industry; the much expanded system of deferred benefits; the ever increasing proportion of workers who own their own homes; the considerable prejudice of management against the hiring of older workers; the marked degree to which skills are company-bound, rather than transferable throughout the economy. These are some of the realities which set the framework for the current struggle about management's freedom of action.

We can readily see that employees are more vulnerable today than heretofore because they are more likely to work for a large organization with multiple plants in which management is constantly expanding some and reducing or closing others. As fixed investments in plant and equipment become relatively less important, as in the new electronics industry, the costs of closing down and relocating are correspondingly reduced. And, in the face of increasing competition among local governments, especially in the South and other chronically surplus manpower areas, to attract new industry through special inducements, the vulnerability of many workers to sudden loss of employment is heightened.

Similarly, workers are increasingly vulnerable as a result of the steady progress of science and technology. Because of technological change, a great many long-term employees can no longer feel secure about their jobs. The number of jobs in the manufacturing sector as a whole did not grow over the past decade; yet a markedly larger output of goods was obtained. Not only does technological advance place jobs in jeopardy, it threatens skills as well. The distinctive new quality of the present acceleration of knowledge and its applications is the speeded up obsolescence of skill and know-how. In earlier days, a journeyman worker had his skill for life. Today, with basic technologies undergoing such rapid changes, his skills are likely to become obsolescent within a decade unless he makes special efforts to refurbish them.

Workers are further threatened by the increasing efforts of business to improve the process of management itself. This results in corresponding disruptions of established work processes and pattern. In many organizations, one or more staff units is employed in attempting to devise new and better ways of utilizing the corporation's capital and manpower. Their aim is to change existing patterns for new and more efficient ones. This effort is specifically directed to economizing in the use of people.

Finally, there is the paradox of the growing affluence of the workingman. Early in this century, when there was plenty of work, an unskilled worker in good health was not much concerned if he had to leave one employer and find another. Unless he was blacklisted or had some other specific employment handicap, it was often a matter of indifference to him whether he remained with one employer or found another. Today, he has much more to lose. The multiple advantages of seniority, which represent his insurance against all but very pervasive unemployment or plant closure, also give him a choice among better paying jobs, preferred claim to overtime, and selection of shifts. In addition, because of extended years of service, he is likely to enjoy longer vacations, a higher pension after retirement, and other valuable benefits. Thus, if his employment in the plant or company is placed in jeopardy, he stands to lose not only the equities that he has built up by working for one employer for a long period of time but also perhaps his savings which he may have invested in a house. In the face of a shutdown, a senior worker may lose all or a good part of his accumulations over a lifetime.

Small wonder therefore that workers, through their unions, have been making ever stronger efforts to restrict the functions of management so that the accumulated rights and benefits of the employees garnered slowly over many years cannot be unilaterally reduced or destroyed.

In actual fact, there has been no fundamental restriction in the scope of management's rights in the areas that have been reviewed—location, subcontracting, and process change. Few unions seriously claim that management does not have the right to locate where it will, subcontract if it will, increase its efficiency if it has the will, or purchase new machinery and make appropriate reductions in its work force. Today, as yesterday, these are management's rights and prerogatives. What has been changing is the price that management must pay for the continued exercise of these rights. It cannot deny the stipulations of its current contract nor can it ignore the substantial rights and benefits that workers have acquired over the years. It cannot use technological innovation to escape from long-standing commitments. Management has the unquestioned right to manage but the advantages which it seeks to gain for the enterprise may not grow out of failure to honor the rights held by workers. Its rights and prerogatives remain as broad as ever. However, when it exercises them today, it must assume some of the costs previously borne entirely by the worker. Some see this as a loss of management rights; but this is an error. The society is constantly changing; the economy is being transformed; workers enter employment with a higher level of education and with aspirations and goals quite different from those of their parents and grandparents. In the face of these radical changes, management cannot possibly discharge its functions effectively by a rigid adherence to a body of rights that reflect an earlier period and different conditions. Management can meet the new challenges which it confronts and those which it will encounter in the future only as it demonstrates flexibility in the exercise of its functions that will enable it to keep the company vital and profitable as the boundaries over rights—its rights, the rights of workers, and the rights of the government—continue to shift. Static rights are incompatible with an expanding economy and a dynamic society.

11. The Job Belongs to the Worker

The classical economists, whatever their strengths and weaknesses, were responsible for an amazing piece of historical generalization when they described the competitive market as the natural way to organize an economy and society. It may have been a preferred way but it surely was not the accustomed way. Right up to the beginning of the nineteenth century, England had many of the hallmarks of a society based, in Sir Henry Maine's words, on status rather than contract.

Status certainly governed the relationships of the vast majority of the citizenry who still lived and worked on the land of their employers. Most farmers were tenants. They paid a set or variable rent in money or in kind or in a combination of both. Occasionally, they also had to work for their landlord for a stipulated number of days in the year. But the employment relationship was not limited to specific obligations. It was much broader. Most landowners, especially those with large estates and whose family had been landowners for many generations, possibly centuries, assumed that they had a continuing obligation to take care of "their" families in bad years as in good, in sickness as in health. Landowner and tenant farmer had a long-term understanding. It was not subject to sudden dissolution.

This pattern still prevails today in many parts of the world, including even the United States, in some areas below the Mason-Dixon line. In some underdeveloped economies, then, even if the farm population conventionally lives at a very low level, they enjoy a type of social security. They may not be able to eat properly or obtain proper medical care but they do have a modicum of security by virtue of free use of a house, land for farming, and, in an emergency, seed or food.

The growth of modern industrialism especially in capitalistic societies dissolved the ties that bound workers and their employers to each other. Thereafter, individuals were on their own—to drive the best bargain they could but with no claims beyond those growing out of the employment contract. The early economists thought highly of the potentialities of the new system, for they correctly percevied that it would contribute to speeding the rate of growth of the economy far beyond that achieved by an agricultural society based on status. But they failed to note, or at least to delineate, the sizable risks that workers soon had to confront since they no longer could look to their employer for even the minimum requirements for survival. While the new industrialization certainly opened up many opportunities for capitalists and workers alike to improve their circumstances, it greatly increased the costs to those who were unable to keep pace or who were victimized by it.

Under the decisions of the courts, a man's property came to be viewed as an extension of himself and, therefore, subject to very wide-ranging protections. The leitmotiv of the nineteenth century and the early part of the twentieth, especially in Anglo-American countries, was the broadening and deepening of the scope and scale of action reserved to the individual. But the worker was generally a man without property. Unless he was able to find a man of property who needed to have work done, he might go hungry. He had first to sell his labor to an employer who wanted to hire him and then he could purchase the essentials for survival—food, clothing, housing.

The only "right" he had was the right to sell his labor and

in the exercise thereof many initially contended that it was illegal and immoral for the state to interfere even to the extent of setting minimum conditions that sought to protect his health and life. But government was slowly but surely forced to become more active. Legislation finally shifted from the shoulders of the individual workingman to the employer or to the community responsibility for covering some of the most serious risks faced by workingmen. Compensation was provided for work accidents or injuries, and later on benefits were provided for unemployed or retired workers.

More important transformations occurred within the free market itself. This was the direct result of the efforts of groups of workers who succeeded in altering the range of freedom available to the employer in contracting for labor. The efforts of workers to establish unions for a long time ran afoul of the law which judged such efforts to be criminal and later civil conspiracies aimed at the destruction of the employer's property. Efforts at unionization were also thwarted or slowed by employers' throwing into the conflict all resources at their command—from the manipulation of public opinion, through bribery of officials, to the use of force.

But labor persevered and eventually broke the stranglehold that employers for so long had over the major organs of society —press, courts, political parties, law enforcement agencies. In the United States, this was done only during major emergencies. The first was the entrance of this country into World War I; the second followed the public's disenchantment with the prevailing economic system after the blistering depression of the early 1930s which paved the way for the radical legislation of the New Deal.

The continuing pressure exercised by many segments of the laboring population to gain a voice in the determination of the employment contract was much more than the work of professional agitators who saw an opportunity to rise on the shoulders of the masses. There was deep and widespread conviction among workers of every description and circumstance that they had a great deal to gain from influencing the conditions governing the terms of their employment. Although the conventional interpretation of trade union activity stresses the prominent place of higher wages and shorter hours on the agenda of labor, these were only two of the priority objectives. Equally important— and, in many cases, even more important—was the workingman's interest in establishing limits on the employer's right to discipline and on his right to disregard seniority in making determinations about promotions, layoffs, and discharges.

In seeking to place these continuing efforts of labor into perspective, we must consider several crucial developments in the larger society which provide considerable illumination both of labor's targets and its relentless efforts to achieve them.

Despite the contributions of the self-regulating market to increasing the standard of living and speeding economic growth for the population as a whole, the workingman found that it had many drawbacks and shortcomings as far as his role as a supplier of labor was concerned. He could not be indifferent to such matters as to the bankruptcy of his employer, one way in which the market squeezed out high cost producers; or to the ebb and flow of business activity, fluctuations appeared to be of the essence of capitalistic enterprise; or to technological change, the driving force on which economic expansion and cost reductions were based; or to unrestricted immigration, which in the United States supplied the great accretions of labor required for the industrialization of the country. For the efficient businessman or the scholar who helped to interpret the structure and mechanisms of a business society, these mechanisms had much to commend them at least in the long run. But for the worker who faced the continuing necessity of getting and holding a job and who, as Keynes said, would be dead in the long run, these regulatory devices in the market place were a bane. His intellect and his emotions told him that in an economy and society in which depression, bankruptcy, obsolescence were imbedded, his self-interest demanded that he seek to moderate the influence and impact of these untoward forces on his job. The fact that he was accused by businessman and professor alike of violating the dictates of laissez-faire impressed the worker not at all. He noted that employers always were engaged in restricting their output whenever it served to increase profits.

His vulnerability was not limited even to these general economic trends. He also had to cope with the exigencies resulting from personal misfortune which might reduce his ability to earn a living as well as with the arbitrary exercise of power of his employer who could discharge him without cause or for minor infractions of rules and thereby destroy the advantages which he had slowly gained over the years as a result of faithful work, faithfully performed.

In its efforts to reduce and if possible, eliminate, much of its vulnerabilities, labor received reenforcement from the fact that as managers replaced owners as the executives of large enterprises, they quickly set about establishing elaborate benefit systems to reward executives who devoted their lives to the corporation. With this model before them, labor redoubled its efforts to secure similar considerations for those who worked at jobs below the executive level.

There was a further spill-over. Trends in the political arena were operating to give increasing meaning to the core elements in our democratic tradition. More and more of the gross differences among citizens were being eliminated or modified. It was not possible for democratic values, principles, and practices to gain strength in the political area without exercising some impact on the world of industry. Too much of a man's life was tied up with his job to permit him to be indifferent about its impact on the totality of his life. Changes in either area affected the other.

Other forces further encouraged workers to seek to influence the terms on which they sold their labor and performed their work. In the early days of industrial capitalism, the worker who acquired skill had the opportunity to exploit it. His knowledge and his competence were part of him. If and when he changed jobs, he took his specialized capital—his skill—with him. But the advent of extreme specialization has altered the nature of skill. Many workmen develop a know-how and a high order of competence that is very valuable, but only to their present employer. If they were to shift jobs, their special competence might be of little or no value to another employer.

A closely related development has been the acceleration in the obsolescence of skills because of the greater investments that society and industry are making in research and development which, in turn, are resulting in more speedy changes in technology.

In the face of these developments affecting the role of skill, it is scarcely surprising that workers have become even more interested in reducing the possibilities of their being summarily discharged or removed from preferred jobs where they have been able to earn higher wages. The emphasis which the unions have long placed on seniority has thus been further reinforced. To round out this picture, it should be noted that the acquisition of skill in the United States has come to depend increasingly on job progression and in-service training rather than on formal apprenticeship. This helps to explain why unions have pressed so strongly for seniority to govern bidding for jobs and training when they become available.

So much for the broad picture. The heart of the matter lies in the fact that labor knows that if employers have a free hand in matters of discipline, promotion, layoff, and recall, then the worker has no protection other than that afforded him by the competitive market. The market has seldom been able to assure employment for all who seek work. Workers have therefore sought to limit, confine, and restrict the power of the employer to determine the terms of employment.

Effective influence on the terms of employment led to renewed and intensified efforts of labor to have a voice in the manner in which work is carried on within the shop. As long as the employer retained the exclusive power to set work norms and rest periods, to discipline, and to make other basic determinations about the way in which work was to be performed, workers would indeed be not his contractual equals but his factotums. Here, then, is one of the most important arenas where the workingman seeks to have his vote count. Important as is the wage that he earns and the hours that he must devote to earning it so are the conditions and circumstances under which he labors.

This dimension of the employment situation inevitably gains in importance as the economy becomes more affluent and the question of a living wage and reasonable hours of work fade more into the background. Next in importance to earning a living wage is a satisfactory working relationship. One of the strengths of a democratic society is the opportunity it offers all citizens to improve the condition of their lives. Small wonder that the workingman is utilizing this freedom to seek to improve the conditions under which he spends so much of his time and his energy.

The efforts of labor have been directed toward improving

basic facets of the employment relationship. In the first place, workers sought to protect their jobs. Second, they have sought a voice in the determination of the amount of effort that they were required to expend in their work. And third, they have sought to increase the rewards which accrue to them by virtue of their work.

The conventional collective bargaining agreement specifies the major conditions under which workers agree to work and in turn commits the employer to provide these conditions. Even in the face of an agreement, no employer is under any compulsion to keep his plant operating and his workers employed if business falls off, a strike prevents his receiving essential components, a breakdown occurs in his machinery, or if any other of the multiple exigencies of production or marketing interfere with his profitable operation. But the contract does bind him not to initiate actions aimed at eliminating jobs or reducing wages through innovations that are not necessitated by either a change in technology or a dislocation in the market place. Of course, the contract does not prevent him from consulting with the union's representatives to determine jointly whether changes might be introduced that would contribute to the economic viability of the company without loss to the worker. The contract simply limits the scope of unilateral action. In a literal sense, his managerial prerogatives have been restricted. However, a collective bargaining agreement—or contract—like every mutual undertaking represents the exchange of a quid for a quo. While the employer's freedom of action has been narrowed in some respects, so too has that of the workers. For instance, they usually relinquish the right to strike during the course of the contract; they forego seeking changes in the terms of the agreement; and they pledge to cooperate in furthering the aims of the enterprise.

Since job security is the core of the worker's interest in the agreement, arbitrators usually hold management to a rather strict interpretation of the contract when it comes to taking actions which will result in the elimination of jobs. They usually uphold management only if there has been an unequivocal change in technology, product line, or market or if other substantial alterations have occurred which necessitate effecting economies in the work force.

But even when management is upheld by the arbitrator in reducing or changing jobs, it must adhere strictly to the prevailing rules of seniority. It cannot simply dismiss those directly affected by the change. Management must follow the contract's provisions with respect to seniority, which may mean the reassignment of a considerable number of workers so that those with the greatest claim on a job retain theirs. In a labor force reduction and bumping process, management must absorb the costs involved in letting trained workers go and providing proper training for the older workers who are then being placed in new jobs. It often is not enough to offer a worker with seniority just one new job and training opportunity and, if he fails, to discharge him. More likely, management must offer him a series of opportunities before it can conclude that there is no suitable work that he can learn to perform satisfactorily.

In the event, that, because of age or other reasons, a worker can no longer meet the demands of his job, he cannot be summarily dismissed as happened to thousands and even millions of men prior to the establishment of collective bargaining agreements. In earlier years, it was entirely within the province of the employer to decide whether or not he would attempt to find alternative employment for a man who had served him long and faithfully but who was no longer capable of meeting the demands of his job. Today, most employers are under contractual obligation to make a conscientious effort to reassign such a worker. Only after such an effort has been made and has failed will action to discharge be upheld.

Much of the insecurity that workers experience results not from the elimination of their jobs or their inability to continue to meet acceptable performance standards but from seasonal and cyclical fluctuations in employment which may put them out of work for a week, a month, or, in the advent of a serious recession, for many months or even years. Among the most valued aspects of security to the worker are the rules which the employer must follow in determining who should be laid off first and who should be recalled first. Except in periods of severe depression or when a company is faced with a long term decline in its work force, employees of fifteen or more years' service are not likely to be exposed to market fluctuations in the demand for labor. This represents the most valuable type of insurance against unemployment.

The second area in which workers have sought through collective bargaining to play a significant role in determining the conditions under which they work is the setting of work standards. No employer is required to keep an inefficient worker on his payroll, but the arbitrators have made it clear that the simple finding that an employee is not performing satisfactorily is not of and by itself ground for discharge—especially if the employee has many years of service. One of the questions that the arbitrators insist on exploring is whether the worker has had competent supervision. The efficiency of the worker is considered not solely in terms of his competence but in the broader context of the work situation including the competence of the managers themselves. Management must manage; it must provide direction, support, and guidance for its work force. If it fails to do this either because of lack of interest, competence, or training, it has the responsibility for any later shortfall in the quantity or quality of the work performed by its employees.

As indicated earlier, management also has an obligation to provide adequate training opportunities. Many contracts contain explicit provisions about the number of hours of training required for different types of jobs, and, in the absence of objective criteria, the arbitrator will usually be sympathetic to grievances claiming that training was too short or otherwise unsatisfactory. When a worker is discharged, he loses not only his job but all the valuable rights that he has accumulated as a result of seniority. This must, in fairness, be the result only of shortcomings on the part of the worker. If management neglects to take any one of the multiple actions that might prevent such failure, it will not be permitted to discharge the worker.

Poor performance, especially if adequate warnings have been given, will of course lead to discharge. But the steady accretion of benefits that workers with long service enjoy have led arbitrators to exercise great caution before they will uphold the discharge of senior workers. The arbitrator usually assumes that long service is proof that the worker has been efficient and otherwise satisfactory.

The arbitrator also assumes that a worker with substantial seniority appreciates the importance of doing his job satisfactorily so as not to jeopardize his valuable rights. Therefore, if such a worker begins to slack off, the arbitrator is likely to look beneath the surface in order to ferret out any special circumstances. If he discovers that the worker is under special types of personal stress or that the fall-off in work followed a recent transfer within the plant, or that the worker is in constant conflict with the foreman, or the existence of some other "extenuating circumstance," the arbitrator is likely to recommend discipline short of discharge. He surmises, and in most instances the future proves him right, that a worker's poor performance for a

few weeks, following upon a long record of satisfactory or superior performance, reflects some special rather than chronic incapacity. He usually decides that it is an implicit obligation of
management to take this into account and to give the worker
another chance. The way in which management goes about the
task of assessing a worker's performance weighs heavily with
the arbitrator in determining whether or not to uphold a decision to discharge. A major and continuing effort of trade unions
has been to reduce, restrict, and eliminate management's scope
for arbitrary action. This grows out of its long experience which
taught it that through arbitrary action management could reward employees who were friendly to it and punish those who
were active on behalf of the union. The very survival of trade
unions requires vigilance, for there are always managements
that would welcome an opportunity to escape from continuing
their relationship with a union. The charge of poor workmanship, unless subject to check and review, could provide management with an easy way of getting rid of the more active union
members. But once a system has been introduced to protect
the few, it is likely to serve as an umbrella for the many. Thus,
many workers, whose performance was held by management as
unsatisfactory and were discharged, were reinstated because the
arbitrators were dissatisfied with the criteria used by management to reach a conclusion about poor workmanship. Arbitrators
usually insist that the standards be objective, that they be objectively applied, and that they be applied to all workers alike.
Then, and only then, are they likely to uphold management in
its decision to discharge a worker for inefficiency.

We have so far considered how workers, through collective
bargaining agreements and through grievances processed under
them, have sought to protect themselves from the loss of jobs.
A related facet of the employment relationship has likewise been

the source of considerable negotiation and arbitration; these are the issues that arise out of clauses and interpretations involving earnings and other benefits. From the worker's point of view, there is, of course, a close relation between the amount of effort required of him and the rewards to which he is entitled. Many cases, therefore, have arisen about the setting and, even more, about the changing of work norms and pay schedules. Since the contract between the union and the employer usually covers both conditions of work and pay, disagreements usually arise if management seeks to alter either the work load or the way in which earnings are calculated. Even if management has hired a consulting firm to undertake a time and motion study before it moves to introduce changes, it may not satisfy the arbitrator. Arbitrators have learned that there is a wide gap between the employment of scientific gadgets or gadgeteers and the emergence of valid results. In general, they will accept results where the union has been party to such a study. In many cases, where this has not been the case, they will appoint their own experts.

The same logic which requires management to negotiate with the union in changing work norms and pay rates also covers working rules. These practices of the shop and the trade play a large role in determining how employees work and what they are able to earn. The origin of many of these work rules is often shrouded in the past but while their legitimacy is sometimes questionable they are for the most part clearly understood by both management and labor. Consequently they are generally protected by the agreement. Therefore, they cannot be altered unilaterally.

In recent years, more and more managements—in steel, railroading, theatrical enterprises, trucking—have complained about the way in which work rules interfere with efficient and economical operations. They tend to slide over the fact that in previous negotiations many of these work rules were proposed and accepted by employers or workers. They represent valuable assets and are not likely to be given away except for equivalent consideration. Harry Bridges bargained the work rules on stevedoring on the West Coast for approximately $25 million. His members had secured these rules through earlier agreements, and like good businessmen, they were now willing to sell their "property" for an appropriate consideration.

In addition to the fact that workers place high value on the local practices of the trade because they are used to them and consider them an integral part of the job, they understand that any change may result in their having to work longer or harder, or that they will earn less for the same amount of effort. Work rules can be changed but the changes must be bargained for; no employer can hope to get rid of onerous rules just because they are onerous any more than any union can contemplate establishing a new rule without proving that it will cost management nothing or that management will gain an equivalent compensation.

While the major advantage of seniority relates to job security, it is also an important determinant of extra earnings. Overtime is an essential element in efficient operations. It provides management with flexibility to meet fluctuating work loads. With overtime pay calculated at time and a half or double the base rate, the amount of overtime pay that a worker is able to earn can mean the difference between a modest and a comfortable standard of living. Therefore, the rules governing the allocation of overtime work are an important part of most collective bargaining agreements. Not every worker who is offered the opportunity to work overtime will want to. But it is his right to have the opportunity in accordance with the terms of the agreement.

Arbitrators are careful to protect this right for they know that many men decide between jobs on the basis of prospective over-time. Any unilateral change which threatens their ability to earn overtime is likely to be viewed by the arbitrator as a violation of an agreement similar to management action to reduce wage rates.

Since workers increasingly are guaranteed certain holidays with pay and vacations of usually two to three weeks under the same contract that establishes their base pay and the conditions for overtime, arbitrators are careful to insure that all of these benefits are protected and that in granting one the employer does not eliminate another. The greatest difficulties arise with respect to vacations, for many contracts stipulate that the worker's preference as to when he goes on vacation will be considered, however, management must likewise be in a position to schedule vacations so as to avoid undue disruption of its production schedules. To complicate this matter, a high proportion of all workers prefer to take their vacations during the summer months. In the face of a clause in the contract which stipulates that workers' preferences as to the time of their vacation will be given consideration, arbitrators will hesitate to uphold a plant shut-down during a slack season as meeting the requirement of choice. It may be more efficient for management to plan for a shut-down but it is not more beneficial for workers to be deprived of choice as to the timing of their vacations.

Arbitrators have come to realize that one of the major satisfactions that workers seek is to be able to plan and order their lives off the job. Many fringe benefits, such as holidays and vacations, contribute substantially to expanding the opportunities of workers to obtain greater satisfactions from the use of their time off the job but they must be able to plan ahead. Hence most arbitrators are willing to agree to protecting their freedom of choice in timing their vacations. On balance, collective bargaining has tended not only to regularize the demands made on a worker at work; it has also gone far to protect his time off the job from arbitrary incursions by his employer.

We have briefly reviewed the many ways in which the worker has gained an increasing role in determining the conditions under which he works and the rewards which he receives. What is the overall impact of these developments? The time is long past when management can deal with labor as with other resources and unilaterally introduce changes with an aim of increasing productivity in disregard of rights of the workers. The existence of a collective bargaining agreement explicitly or implicitly provides that most changes involving workers must be jointly agreed to by management and the union. While management frequently considers consultation and negotiation as a restriction of its ability to manage, it often stands to gain by such actions. Workers know a great deal about what goes on in the shop and surely know better than others what they want. It may be that management is still at an early stage of learning how to profit from the advantages inherent in a consultative process but there are advantages, as well as disadvantages. Arbitrators repeatedly point out to management the gains that they might have made had they taken the trouble to seek the opinion and the help of the union before they initiated or altered a particular policy.

Management has found it difficult to share power. Its inclination is to go it alone. And, yet, it has much to gain from learning how to work cooperatively with labor, not only because it must but because of the potential contributions that labor can make to the heightened efficiency and profitability of the company.

The last decades have witnessed not only a shift in power but a shift in the division of the profits between management and labor. The power of organized labor, supported by a friendly government and public, has been sufficient to alter the way in which costs are calculated and earnings are divided. Many of the real costs that the individual laborer formerly was forced to absorb have now been transferred to the employer's account or to the account of the community. Nor is there any end to this process in sight. The latest development has been that arbitrators and the courts have recognized that a worker has a property right in his job by virtue of years of faithful service and the many benefits that attach thereto. The employer cannot escape responsibility by the simple device of relocating his plant. This may look like a radical innovation in legal philosophy but in point of fact it is simply an extension of a straight line trend. Employers have recognized that men who have served them long and faithfully are entitled to various types of deferred benefits—particularly pensions, separation wages, paid-up insurance. Nothing is more valuable to a worker than the right to his job and the protection of his seniority. Those who sit in judgment about the changing equities of the worker and management have sought to limit the opportunities of management to destroy such valuable rights.

The multiple developments reviewed in this chapter must appear to those concerned solely with managerial rights and employers' costs as actions which can only have a severely limiting effect on the performance of the free market. It is easy to jump from this conclusion to the generalization that these limitations will be reflected in higher prices, lower profits, and slower growth.

And well they may. But there is no certainty that they will. The American economy has long been characterized by relatively high wages but these have not stood in the way of many companies competing successfuly in the markets of the world. The crucial issue always is the response of management and labor to new constraints and new opportunities. There is overwhelming evidence from our history that improved conditions of work are a stimulus, not a deterrent, to economic progress.

In any one industry or in any short period of time, costs that have come to be assessed against management as a result of the expanding control exercised by labor over work may not be fully compensated for by increases in productivity. But a society in which workers are freed from many insecurities incident to employment, where they have acquired dignity and freedom, and where they have gained the right to play a significant role in determining the conditions of their employment is a better society than one in which they are fully exposed to the vagaries of the free market.

Within the purview of the larger sweep of history, the current transformations are easy to understand. That stage of industrial capitalism in which workers lost all control over their jobs was unique. There was no counterpart in any prior society and it is unlikely that any future society will provide a parallel. Jobs have always been to a considerable degree under the control of those who filled them. This is likely to continue to be the pattern in the future.

12. The Reach of Democracy

The legitimizing of laissez-faire resulted in restrictions and restraints being placed on a democratic society's experimenting with the development of new forms of governmental activity. In the face of the new premise that the best of all societies was one in which the optimum amount of decision-making is reserved to the individual, social reformers found it hard to convince the body politic that there were advantages to be gained by strengthening the governmental arm. The newly entrenched doctrine of individual self-determination placed a major barrier in the path of collective action. The only exceptions related to religious, social, and eleemosynary efforts. Since these voluntary organizations did not want to alter in any significant regard the structures involved in the making of goods and the making of money, they were allowed wide latitude for growth.

But whenever a group of citizens decided to organize for the specific purpose of introducing a significant change into the way in which production was organized, labor was sold, or consumers spent their income there was an outcry from the conservative leaders of society who warned that any deviation from the logic of the free market could lead only to dire consequences. The conservatives warned that such reformist efforts would fly in the face of both logic and experience. The aims of the reformers might be commendable but sentimentality could not emerge victorious in a struggle with reality. Reality, contended these conservative leaders, was that the self-interest of the individual was a much better foundation for social organization than the centralization of power and control in the hands of a small autocracy or a democratic political machine.

The conservatives had two strong anchors—the one economic, the other political. They argued that the free market insured that the economy would make the best use of available resources and then sought to demonstrate that the same principles that furthered economic welfare strengthened political freedom. The strength of the conservative position was greatly enhanced, especially in the United States after the Civil War, by the unequivocal evidence of progress on both fronts—economic and political. However, while the progress was real, the policies which contributed to it were frequently in violation of the basic tenets of laissez-faire. But the ideology was strongly entrenched and it was reenforced by the power that the conservatives were able to exercise through the press, politics, and the market place to thwart most efforts to alter the basic institutional framework and establish a counterpoise to the free and untrammeled exercise of power by property owners.

But changes slowly did occur both on the governmental and industrial fronts—changes that were in no small measure the outgrowth of the progress made possible in the economic and political realms under the regimen of free enterprise and political democracy.

The very promises made by the defenders of the status quo turned out to be a spur to reform. Their insistence on a system of allowing maximum scope for individual initiative established a benchmark against which to measure the shortcomings of the economy and society. And there were serious defects. Nor were there automatic mechanisms to correct them. The free labor market, for instance, did not put an end to sweatshops, company towns, periodic unemployment, or other conditions that habitually or periodically caused widespread misery among the mass of the working population. The continuing gap between promise and accomplishment therefore acted as a burr.

So, too, did the extension of political democracy. Shortly after the end of the Civil War, all groups, including the recently emancipated slaves, were enfranchised. Although during the succeeding decades, more and more southern Negroes were in one way or another prevented from voting, almost every other male inhabitant except Orientals and Indians was permitted to vote, many before they had become citizens. It became increasingly difficult for those who warned about the evils of governmental interference to beat down reformist trends in the face of the broadened political franchise. Slowly but surely, the proponents of non-interference had to give way, first on local and state fronts where action was taken to institute controls affecting the health of the community, and then with respect to action aimed more specifically at reforms of the work place.

The expansion of free public education also increased the potential for reform as more and more of the immigrants and the children of immigrants shared in the American dream. The school contributed mightily to the spread of the dominant value structure with its emphasis on economic progress and self-fulfill-ment. Consequently, those who found that they were unable to earn a living wage or to extricate themselves from the adverse circumstances into which they had been born and bred, as well as those who were dissatisfied with their progress sought for new and better ways to see their dream fulfilled. They became a potent force for change.

Finally, the conservative ethos was made more vulnerable by the impact of the technological and managerial transformations that were occurring within industry itself. The preconditions of an individualistic society and economy predicated on the self-determination of the farmer and tradesman were being rapidly submerged by the rapid aggrandizement of the large corporate unit with its increasing reliance on a hired management. The concentration of ever larger numbers of workers under one industrial roof; the application of scientific management to the process of production; and the general ruthlessness of policies affecting employees all operated as a spur and goad to the organizational efforts of workers who hoped that through pooling their strength they might be able to cushion and moderate some of the harshness of the market place. Unlike workers in many European countries, American workers had little interest in a radical transformation of the society. Their main objective was to secure as many of the vaunted benefits and blessings of capitalism as quickly as possible. In their eagerness to acquire and enjoy the good things of life, they did not hesitate to throw over one or another idol. But they were pragmatists who wanted to make American capitalism work better, not revolutionists who sought to topple the system. They were in search of the good society and they wanted to be full members in good standing.

We have seen the inherent contradiction between a true political democracy and the maintenance of a policy of laissez-faire once the economy became transformed from one of small independent enterprises to one of large corporate units in which the mass of the population had to sell its labor. Without a democratic tradition, as in Germany and Japan, workingmen might not have been very happy with their share of the spoils but they would not do very much about it, since the dominant group in society saw that they were permitted to enjoy substantial benefits both in terms of personal consumption and in terms of the psychic benefits of a strident nationalism. The situation was quite different in the United States where the majority could make its will felt through the polls. While, in many parts of Western Europe, the working classes had to struggle during the latter half of the nineteenth century and the early years of this century for political freedom, the American laborer faced a different challenge. He had to decide how best to make use of the political freedom which he had already won. Paradoxically, he did not focus his primary attention on the political arena. He saw the industrial battlefield as the one where victory could be won and it was here that he directed his attention. His major objective on the political front was to establish a neutrality on the part of the courts and the police so that he would not be continuously overwhelmed in his struggle with management.

American workers early came to understand that the value of political freedom was to be tested not only by what happened once in four years at the time of a presidential election but every day that they went to work for an employer who exercised substantial power over them. Freedom had little meaning if most of one's waking hours are spent at the whim of another.

The American industrial laborer early came to appreciate the indivisibility of political freedom and economic independence. This was directly in line with the American tradition; this had guided the "Founding Fathers" when they drafted the Constitution. It was modern management, with its aggressive technology, finance, markets and politics, that was the radical force that changed the face of agricultural America.

As the ballot was the worker's guarantee that he would be able to make his voice heard in the political arena, the trade union was the instrument that he fashioned to exercise power on the industrial front. It was to the union that he looked to expand and protect his equities in the job market. If he was to enjoy a good life as a free citizen, he had to take action to improve his wage, reduce his job insecurity, and otherwise make himself less vulnerable to the dictates of his employer. Freedom off the job was incompatible with slavery on the job.

But it was easier to join the issue than to resolve it. For the exercise of the rights of management that labor set out to restrict, restrain and reduce were intimately associated with the functions of management and therefore with the efficiency and growth of the economy. While labor strove to expand the worker's equity in his job, management continued to strive to keep the business competitive, earn profits, and provide satisfactory outlets for retained earnings. The real struggle during the past several decades has been to modify the respective rights and duties of both management and labor in such a fashion as to facilitate the accretion of equities to the workingman without fundamentally placing in jeopardy the underlying efficiency of the enterprise.

Let us shift from our consideration of the broad trends in the economy and society to the narrow frame within which employers and employees have worked out their accommodations and have developed what the Supreme Court has called a system of industrial self-government within which arbitration plays a crucial role. The following observations will identify the core problems and outline how they have come to be handled as a result of the pulling and hauling between management and labor.

The first point to note is the necessity that large organizations commit their rules and regulations to paper. In no other way can successive levels of managers, many of them located hundreds or thousands of miles from headquarters, receive the guidance they need to discharge their responsibilities in dealing with the men under their control. Large organizations must exert continuing pressure to substitute the formal and the objective for the informal and personal in the realm of labor relations as with so many other facets of their policy.

Once a union is established within a company and management must bargain with it, there is no escaping the necessity of a written contract which must at least contain the key terms of the agreement. A written contract is an inevitable conclusion to an agreement, but a contract alone cannot serve. Since it is never possible to spell out all of the eventualities that may arise during the life of the contract, the written document must be limited to the key issues. How then do the parties determine their respective rights and know the other's responsibilities on issues which have not been covered explicitly? Here is where arbitration comes in. Since both management and labor have an interest in the steady flow of work, neither can permit each disagreement to lead to a work stoppage—either through a lockout or a strike. On the other hand the final power of labor to effect a change in the rights and duties of management is through resort to striking. Consequently, for labor to agree not to strike during the term of a contract, it must be assured that its claims will be objectively considered and expeditiously acted on. This is a task that labor, as management, has been willing to have performed by the arbitrator since each has a voice in his selection. Since the arbitrator usually continues to act only as long as each of the principals is satisfied with the objectivity of his decisions, each runs, at best, a limited risk.

There are further safeguards that surround the process although some are more theoretical than real. The arbitrator's role is to interpret the contract, which means that he should not add to or subtract from the terms agreed upon. The fact that his duties are thus limited means that a third independent factor is not introduced into the relationships worked out between the two parties. But there is a point beyond which this restraint breaks down. Life cannot always be easily fit into pre-established categories. Even very long and elaborate contracts cannot contain all of the contingencies that may arise. As a result, the arbitrator is repeatedly forced to break new ground, guided only by his reading of what has been committed to paper and by what he can learn about prevailing practices. In many instances, the written words and the practices in the work place are clues and no more. The arbitrator must then attempt to find an adjudication that balances the equities that workers are seeking with the never-ending insistence of management that it can keep the firm alive and thriving only if it can uninterruptedly pursue the goal of efficiency.

The arbitrator is allowed great discretion. Although his judgments can on occasion be appealed to the courts, recent decisions by the Supreme Court have indicated very clearly that the judiciary is loath to act as an appellate body. It will surely not enter into the substance of issues nor even the reasoning underlying the decision. The only question that the courts are likely to review is whether, under the terms of the contract, the arbitrator had the right to deal with the grievance. Judicial review is usually limited to questions of arbitratibility, and, even here, the highest court has proceeded with great restraint. Its clear preference is to leave as much scope as possible to the arbitration process and to rely to a maximum on the judgments of the arbitrator. The courts have given increasing evidence of late that their preference is to see the system of arbitration strengthened and relied upon as the principal method for the adjudication of conflicts under collective bargaining.

Nor is this surprising. The semi-judicial methods of arbitration are, after all, more suited to the complexities of the employment situation than are more formal systems of justice. The arbitrator has wide latitude in attempting to elicit evidence and equally wide latitude when it comes to rendering a decision. There is no necessity for him to detail his reasons—although he is likely to do so. Nor is he bound by precedent. In these and many other regards, arbitration is a more flexible method of adjudicating conflicting claims. Since the objective of arbitration is to keep the disagreements between management and labor at a minimum, and, when disagreements do arise, to handle them in a manner that contributes to the major goal of both parties (which is to keep on working and producing); arbitrators are always future-oriented. They must understand the logic of industrial enterprise and they must attempt at all times to render decisions that are in harmony, not in conflict, with this logic.

Although arbitration is informal compared to the judicial process, the written contract, the grievance procedure, and the other mechanisms provided for under the agreement have gone far to introduce due process into the arena of work. This represents a major accomplishment: trials of strength have been increasingly superseded by institutionalized methods of adjudicating conflicting claims.

It is worth noting that despite its informality, arbitration has come to place considerable stress on the adherence to procedure. It is questionable whether equity can be rendered except under a system of rules which both parties must observe. For instance, the fact that workers have the right to grieve under the contract does not mean that they have the right to disobey whenever they decide that the employer is making an unjustified demand. They must comply and then they may grieve, as the arbitrators repeatedly remind them. Only in exceptional situations where a worker's health or life may be endangered may procedure be disregarded. For the aim of the contract is to protect both the worker's rights and management's rights and this can best be done by the worker complying with management's directive and then submitting the contested order to review in a manner which will not disrupt the entire plant.

There are many other ways in which arbitrators have sought to introduce due process into the relationships between management and labor. For instance, while recognizing that management may have the right under the contract to discipline a worker for one or another type of offense, they will not permit management to act in a way which runs counter to the basic values of the community. The arbitrator usually insists that management give clear notice of its intention to punish for a particular infraction of the rules. Although lack of knowledge of the law may not be a valid excuse in civil life, arbitrators are likely to inquire whether a worker who broke a rule could reasonably have been expected to know of it. There is, then, an obligation on the part of management to make known to its employees the types of behavior which are proscribed before it can take disciplinary action. Management may have in the past permitted many rules to be broken with impunity. It cannot arbitrarily or capriciously dust off one or another in order to discipline a particular individual or group of workers. If it intends to tighten discipline and enforce a previously ignored rule, it must make its intent known.

Similarly, arbitrators are sensitive to the fairness with which discipline is administered. Management is not permitted to play favorites. One man must be treated like the next. This does not mean that management is not permitted to discriminate between first offenders and others who are repeated violators but it must deal with like offenders in a like manner. For, in our democratic society, the punishment meted out to men guilty of the same offense must not be arbitrary.

The purpose of industrial discipline is constructive, which means that management uses a progressive range of penalties in order to change the behavior of the worker so that he will be able to work effectively and thereby retain his job. The arbitrator therefore suspects any type of managerial action which smacks of entrapment. Management will not be sustained if it has acted to "get" a man, or frequently even if it has failed to warn him. While management will be upheld in discharging workers who have committed major offenses such as stealing, instigating a fight, or outright insubordination, in the case of others whose failings are less extreme and whose deficiencies have been revealed not in a single incident but over a period of time, the burden is on management to show that it has done its best to help them before resorting to the final penalty of discharge.

There are many other ways in which arbitrators have sought to impress upon both management and labor that the heart of any ordered system of contractual obligations is that it is to the clear advantage of both parties to behave in a manner consistent with the prescribed procedures and with the prevailing standards of fair play. There is nothing to be gained and much to be lost if the disputants become so concerned with victory in a particular case that they act in a way to jeopardize their mutual obligations, not only as signatories to a contract but also as fellow citizens in a democracy.

The evolving system of collective bargaining with its grievance and arbitration procedures has the flexibility which comes not only from the procedural mechanisms for the resolution of conflict but which are inherent in the relatively short-run nature of most agreements. Hence, if either management or labor discovers during the course of a contract that it has agreed to an arrangement that is unduly costly in human or monetary terms, the opportunity will soon arise for reopening the issue. Each party has such an extended list of what it wants to write into the contract as well as what it is determined to keep out that there is considerable room for the shifting of priorties and for the give and take that will eventually assure a more satisfactory agreement. The important point here is that even if one contract involves elements that prove to be particularly disturbing, they can usually be removed in the next contract. The question then becomes whether the party is willing to pay the price for removing an element previously agreed to and which can now only be bargained out of the contract. There is a tendency to put up with a particular arrangement, even if it is a disturbing one rather than pay the price that may be involved in getting rid of it. One result of such dalliance is the slow accretion of many burdensome rules and restrictions that occasionally result in a constellation that can eventually prove to be very burdensome.

Extremists have contended that collective bargaining represents the crucial step in the destruction of management's rights for the union, by its very nature, must seek at the time of each agreement to increase the returns and to widen the protections afforded its members. The result of this can only be a major reduction and limitation on the scope of management.

Several points are worth noting in rebuttal. Much of what management agrees to in a contract, while important to the workingman, does not really affect the heart of the company's operations. Many of the gains that labor is able to make actually cost management little either in money or rights. Second, for everything that an intelligent management agrees to, it receives a return—by far, the most important of these is the willingness of labor to work effectively; it often pledges not to strike throughout the length of the contract. A management that can plan its future operations with the knowledge that there will be no disturbance on the labor front has gained a great deal. But more accrues to management from its contract than assurance of general peace and tranquility. The contract, through its ordered rules and procedures, prevents the eruption of a great many potential issues by providing an institutionalized method for dealing with them. Without a contract, or some other clearly defined set of rules, disagreements could keep an establishment in constant turmoil.

The contract also, of course, places a considerable number of obligations on labor. Failure to meet them can lead to serious penalties. Management retains most of its rights to manage which includes, of course, the direction of the work force. For certain offenses, it has the right to discharge a worker on the spot. It must make all of the crucial decisions involved in expanding or contracting the work force in response to changes in the market. It continues to determine alone whether to buy new equipment that may result in the discharge or reassignment of large numbers of workers. In most instances it remains free to relocate from one region of the country to another. Moreover, if it finds that it has agreed to conditions that prove to be very onerous, it need not live with them indefinitely. It can bargain them out of the contract at a later date.

If the decisions with respect to efficiency of the work force, scale of operations, technological innovation, and relocation remain firmly in the hands of management, how can it be argued that management has been stripped as a result of collective bargaining of its rights to manage? This has not happened.

What, then, has transpired? Simply this. The parameters within which management must function have been altered. It cannot manage as it used to manage. The closer its decisions come to affecting the security and pay of the worker the more carefully it must tread. The same holds for those of its actions that are likely to upset the conditions under which the worker has been accustomed to work. In the past, management was permitted to take many actions which are now denied it. There are even more actions which it must undertake differently. It must now often consult and negotiate before it acts; it must make a serious effort to protect the rights and privileges that workers have acquired under the contract or as a result of custom.

But this is vastly different from the contention that management's rights have been eroded. Its functions remain but in the exercise of them it can no longer rely exclusively on rights which it once possessed. In the intervening years the working-man has acquired various rights as a result of bargaining with management and management must take cognizance of their rights and respect them.

Another way of assessing the role of arbitration in the resolution of conflicts between management and the members of its work force is to consider whether there is any possibility of avoiding such conflicts or whether there are alternative methods for coping with them that would prove more effective from the viewpoint either of the contestants themselves or the larger society. In answer to the first question, the burden of history is unequivocal. There never has been nor is there likely to be the possibility of structuring the process of work so as to avoid conflicts between those who direct it and those who perform it. For short periods of time and in the face of overwhelming emergencies such as war it may be possible for employees to submerge their own values and goals and to submit wholeheartedly to the direction of their supervisors to accomplish a specific end. This may happen also when small groups of dedicated people join together to accomplish a particular goal, be it the furtherance of a religious, charitable, or educational objective or the accomplishment of an overriding political or economic goal. But examples of whole-hearted cooperation in work are few: conflict is indigenous to work in groups no matter what the environment may be—a family, a small independent enterprise, a large organization—or whether the work is carried on under a system of slavery, feudalism, capitalism, socialism, or communism. It does not matter. Conflict cannot be avoided. It can only be differently resolved.

The alternatives for resolution are also limited. Physical power as an instrument of control over workers is costly in the extreme. It requires large numbers of supervisors and it leads to the certainty that workers will devote much time and effort to outwitting them. Since force has limited value as an instrument for the resolution of work conflicts, there remains only one basic alternative—some system for orderly adjudication by an impartial third party, be he judge, arbitrator, or umpire. This explains why even certain non-union firms have established grievance procedures and some methods for resolving disagreements. Many different institutional devices can be used but the variability of techniques is less significant than the fact that they all derive their sanctions from some system of judicial or quasi-judicial adjudication.

Work conflicts arise in the industrial realm but their resolution involves the totality of social forces. The imperatives to which management must respond in its search for efficiency are affected by changes in science, technology and law; and the workers' search for equity is constantly undergoing a metamorphosis as their aspirations and goals change in response to the changes that are affecting their lives—how they are educated, how they live, and, above all, how the dreams of their youth so strongly tinctured with traditional American optimism are reconciled with reality.

There is no surcease from conflict at work, for no man who values his freedom can ever be unconcerned about the conditions under which he constricts it by entering into an employment contract. Moreover the nature of the conflicts will be constantly transformed as a consequence of the dynamic forces that operate on the work situation resulting from changes in technology, the economy, and the people who are employed.

The arbitrator whose responsibility it is to resolve these conflicts is himself a dynamic force operating to alter the environment. His decisions establish yet another constraint within which further conflicts must be assessed and resolved. But, in assessing the evidence which comes before him and in seeking to reach a balanced decision in which considerations of efficiency will be harmonized with those of equity, the arbitrator more frequently than not introduces into the industrial world the new values which have begun to be accepted by the society at large. These new values are introduced not because the arbitrator is an innovator or reformer but as the inevitable by-product of his decision-making. The arbitrator is likely to be attuned to the emerging values of the society and in his assessment of the conflicts that come to him he will draw on them for direction and emphasis. For his decisions must not only be conducive to management's search for efficiency but must be acceptable to the workers in their search for equity.

Thus, the arbitrator becomes unwittingly the instrument for expanding the reach of democracy at the work place. He helps to extend and deepen the area within which democratic values find expression. In this process, he makes a significant contribution to the strengthening of industry and to the expansion of democracy. Since his contribution is the by-product of a basic function recognized as essential by both management and the workers, the fortunes of democracy are advanced. To the extent that the con-

servative tradition is correct in stressing the mutual interdependence of political democracy and economic progress to that
extent does arbitration contribute not only to the efficiency
of the economy but also to the deepening of democracy.

Bibliography

GENERAL REFERENCES

Bendix, R. *Work and Authority: Ideologies of Management in the Course of Industrialization*. New York, John Wiley & Sons, 1956.

Berle, A. *Power Without Property*. New York, Harcourt, Brace & Company, 1959.

Burnham, James. *The Managerial Revolution*. New York, The John Day Company, 1941.

Chamberlain, N. *Collective Bargaining*. 1st ed. New York, McGraw-Hill Book Company, Inc., 1951.

Ginzberg, E. *The House of Adam Smith*. New York, Columbia University Press, 1934.

Golden, C. S., and H. J. Ruttenberg. *The Dynamics of Industrial Democracy*. (Chapter VIII.) New York, Harper & Brothers, 1942.

Gordon, Robert A. *Business Leadership in the Large Corporation*. Berkeley, University of California Press, 1961. (Paper ed. published in cooperation with The Brookings Institution.)

Kerr, C., and L. H. Fisher. "Plant Sociology: The Elite and the Aborigines" in M. Komarovsky, ed., *Common Frontiers of the Social Sciences*. Glencoe, Ill., Free Press of Glencoe, Inc., 1957.

Kornhauser, A., R. Dubin, and A. Ross, eds. *Industrial Conflict*. New York, McGraw-Hill Book Company, Inc., 1954.

Kuhn, J. *Bargaining in the Grievance Process*. New York, Columbia University Press, 1961.

Kuhn, J., and I. Berg. "Bargaining and Work-Rules Disputes." To appear in 1963.

Polanyi, K. *The Great Transformation*. New York, Rinehart & Company, 1944.

Proceedings of Labor Management Conference, New York State School of Industrial and Labor Relations, Cornell University, New York City, February 4, 1960. *The Arbitration of Two "Man-*

agement's Rights" Issues; Work Assignments and Contracting Out.

Slichter, S., J. Healy, and R. Livernash. *The Impact of Collective Bargaining on Management.* Washington, D.C., The Brookings Institution, 1960.

Smith, Adam. *The Wealth of Nations.* New York, Random House (Modern Library Edition), 1937.

Stone, M. *Labor-Management Contracts at Work.* New York, Harper & Brothers, 1961.

Torrence, G. W. *Management's Right to Manage.* Washington, D.C., Bureau of National Affairs, 1959.

Vollmer, H. M. *Employee Rights and The Employment Relationship.* Berkeley, University of California Press, 1960.

REFERENCES TO ARBITRATION

Aaron, B. "Arbitration in the Federal Courts: Aftermath of the Trilogy," *U.C.L.A. Law Review,* IX (1962), 360.

—— "Reflections on the Legal Nature and Enforceability of Seniority Rights," *Harvard Law Review,* LXXV (1962), 1532.

Chandler, M. K. "Management Rights and Union Interests: The Case of Contracting Out," Paper delivered to Labor-Management Seminar, Columbia University Graduate School of Business, Spring, 1962. A selection of materials from a book to be published in 1963 by McGraw-Hill Book Company, Inc.

Cox, A. "Reflections Upon Labor Arbitration," *Harvard Law Review,* LXXII (1959), 1482.

Crawford, D. A. "A Preliminary and Otherwise Rough Draft on 'Contracting Out.' " (Unpublished manuscript).

Davey, H. "The Supreme Court and Arbitration: The Musings of an Arbitrator," *Notre Dame Law Review,* Vol. XXXVI (1961).

Fleming, R. W. "Some Problems of Due Process and Fair Procedure in Labor Arbitration," *Stanford Law Review,* XIII (1961), 235.

Gould, W. B. "The Supreme Court and Labor Arbitration," *Labor Law Journal,* Vol. XII (1961).

Mayer, H. "Arbitration and the Judicial Sword of Damocles" *Labor Law Journal,* IV (1953), 723.

Phelps, O. W. *Discipline and Discharge in the Unionized Firm.* Berkeley, University of California Press, 1959.

Prasow, P. "Reducing the Risks of Arbitration," *California Management Review*, Vol. I (1959).

Shulman, H. "Reason, Contract, and Law in Labor Relations," *Harvard Law Review*, LXVIII (1955), 999.

—— "The Role of Arbitration in The Collective Bargaining Process," *Proceedings*, Conference on Collective Bargaining and Arbitration, Institute of Industrial Relations, University of California, 1949.

Summers, C. "Individual Rights in Collective Agreements—A Preliminary Analysis," *N.Y.U. Twelfth Annual Conference on Labor* 63 (1959).

Taylor, G. W. "Effectuating the Labor Contract Through Arbitration," Washington, D.C., Bureau of National Affairs, 1949.

Torrence, W. D. "More Comments on Union Security and Management Authority," *Labor Law Journal*, Vol. XII (1961).

Updegraff, C. M., and W. P. McCoy. *Arbitration of Labor Disputes.* (2nd ed.), Washington, D.C., Bureau of National Affairs, 1961.

Upton, W. W. "Case Comments on Arbitration," *West Virginia Law Review*, LXIII (1961), 374.

Wallen, S. "Arbitration of Work Assignment Disputes." A paper prepared for delivery at a labor-management institute held in New York City, October 14, 1959, under the auspices of the New York State School of Industrial and Labor Relations, Cornell University.

—— "The Impact of Arbitration on Management and Union Decisions," Paper prepared for delivery at The New England Regional Conference of the National Academy of Arbitrators, Cambridge, Mass., October 17, 1957.

—— "Recent Supreme Court Decisions on Arbitration: An Arbitrator's View," *West Virginia Law Review*, LXIII (1961), 295.

Warren, E. L., and I. Bernstein. "The Arbitration Process," *The Southern Economic Journal*, Vol. XVII (1950).

—— "A Profile of Labor Arbitration," *Industrial and Labor Relations Review*, IV (1951), 200.

Wirtz, W. "Due Process of Arbitration" in *The Arbitrator and the Parties, Proceedings of The Eleventh Annual Meeting, National Academy of Arbitrators*.

Index of Arbitration Cases